AND WOMEN

LESLIE W. LEAVITT

Illustrated by Peter Horne

1800 word vocabulary

LONGMAN

LONGMAN GROUP UK LIMITED
Longman House, Burnt Mill
Harlow, Essex CM20 2JE, England
and Associated Companies throughout the world.

© L. W. Leavitt 1958

All rights reserved; no part of this publication may be
reproduced, stored in a retrieval system, or transmitted
in any form or by any means, electronic, mechanical,
photocopying, recording, or otherwise, without
the prior written permission of the Publishers.

First published 1958
Third impression 1960
New impressions *1962 (twice); *1963 (twice);
*1964 (twice); *1965; *1966 (thrice);
*1967; *1968 (twice); *1969;
*1970 (twice); *1971; *1974;
*1975; *1978; *1979; *1982;
*1984 (twice); *1985;
*1986; *1987 (twice);
*1988 (twice); *1990

ISBN 0-582-53512-3

We are indebted to Miss Eve Curie for permission to base the biography of Madame Curie on her book *Madame Curie*, published by Messrs. William Heinemann Ltd.; to Messrs. Methuen & Co. Ltd. for material from *The Story of Albert Schweitzer*, by Jo Manton; and to the author and Messrs. Constable & Co. Ltd. for material from *Lady in Chief*, by Mrs. Cecil Woodham-Smith, published in Britain by Messrs. Methuen & Co. Ltd. and in America by the McGraw-Hill Book Company Inc. under the title of *Lonely Crusader*.

Words outside stage 5 of the New Method Supplementary
Readers are in a list on page III.

Produced by Longman Group (FE) Ltd
Printed in Hong Kong

Contents

		PAGE
1	Mahatma Gandhi	5
2	Florence Nightingale	18
3	Abraham Lincoln	37
4	Madame Curie	58
5	Albert Schweitzer	82
	Questions on the Stories	105
	List of New Words	111

Mahatma Gandhi

One

MAHATMA GANDHI

On the evening of January 30, 1948, a little old man was slowly crossing the courtyard of his home on his way to prayers. Suddenly the sound of four gun-shots was heard, and the man fell to the ground. That night his great friend, Pandit Nehru, speaking on the radio to the people of India, said: "The light has gone out of our lives and everywhere it is dark." The life-story of this little, old and very great man, Mahatma Gandhi, is one which everyone should know.

His Home

Mohandas Gandhi was born in a city in the west part of India on October 2, 1869. Mohandas was his first name. The word Mahatma means "Great Soul" and is a title which was given him later. For many years members of the Gandhi family had held important government posts, and for a long time the father of Mohandas was chief officer in one of the states of India. The father was a fine and brave man, and very good at his work.

The son loved his father very much, and also his mother. His mother was very serious in her religion and never thought of beginning a meal without prayer. At one time she felt that her religion demanded that she should not eat until she saw the sun. It was then the season of rain, and often the sun was not seen for a long time. Her children were much troubled and spent long hours looking up at the sky to be able to hurry to tell her that the sun was shining and that she could eat.

At School

In his later life Gandhi wrote a book which tells us many things about his early years. In this book he says that it was not easy for him to make friends with other boys in school, and that his only companions were his books and his lessons. He used to run home from school as soon as classes were over for fear that someone would talk to him or make fun of him. As a little boy he was very honest. One day a small event concerned with school games troubled him very much. Because he did not enjoy being with other boys and also because he wanted to help his father after school, he did not like to take part in school games. He thought they were a waste of time.

One day when they had had their classes in the morning only, Mohandas was supposed to return to school at four o'clock for school games. He had no watch and the cloudy weather deceived him. He arrived late; the games were over; the boys had gone home. The next day when he explained to the head of the school why he was late, he was not believed. He was told that he was not telling the truth and that he must be punished. He, Mohandas Gandhi, a liar? No! No! But how could he prove that he was telling the truth? At this early age he began to understand that a man of truth must also be a careful man. Carelessness often leads others to have wrong ideas about a person.

Later Mohandas changed his mind about the value of games in the playground. Fortunately he had read in books that walking was a valuable exercise, and while still a boy began to take long walks in the open air, a form of exercise which he enjoyed and carried on during all his life.

He also says in his book that his handwriting was very poor, and that he did nothing to improve it because he believed that it was not important. Later, when he was in South Africa, he saw the excellent handwriting of lawyers and young men of that country and became ashamed of his own. He saw that bad handwriting should be considered a weakness in a person. When he then tried to improve his own handwriting, he found it was too late.

Marriage

Mohandas was married at the early age of thirteen, which in India at that time was not thought to be too young. The oldest son of the family was already married, and the father and mother decided that the second son and the third son, Mohandas, together with an uncle's son, should all be married at the same time. Marriages, with their presents, dinners, fine clothes and all the rest, cost the families a lot of money, and a marriage of all three together would save much. The young wife of Mohandas had never been to school. This early marriage did not help his lessons, and he lost a year in high school. Fortunately, by hard work he was later able to finish two classes in one year.

Mistakes of Youth

Among his few friends at school was a young man whose character was not very good. Mohandas knew this, but refused to accept the advice of others and felt that he would be able to change the character of his friend. The family of Gandhi belonged to a religious group which did not believe in taking the life of any creature, and so the eating of meat was forbidden them. But Mohandas's friend set out to make him believe that the eating of meat was good for him. He explained it in this way: "We are a weak people. The English are able to rule over us because they eat meat. I myself am strong and a fine runner. It is because I am a meat-eater. You should eat meat, too. Eat some and see what strength it gives you." After a time the young Mohandas partly believed his companion. He himself was certainly not strong and could hardly jump or run. He was afraid of the dark, too, and always had a light burning in his bedroom at night. The desire to eat meat was great, even though he hated to deceive his father and mother. One day the two boys went off to a quiet place by the river alone, and there Mohandas tasted meat, goat meat, for the first time. It made him sick. For about a year after that, from time to time his friend arranged for him to eat meat. At last Mohandas stopped completely, believing that nothing was worse than deceiving his father and mother in this way. They never learned of what he had done, but from that time on through his whole life he never tasted meat again.

At about this time he and another young man began to smoke, not because they really liked it but because they thought that they got pleasure in blowing smoke from their mouths like grown-up men. They had little money to buy cigarettes, and the unsmoked ends of their uncle's cigarettes were not enough. So occasionally they stole a little money from the servants in the house. Mohandas soon gave up smoking, and came to feel that it was dirty and harmful.

These actions of his troubled the young man Mohandas because he had determined to build his life on truth, and he knew that in deceiving his father and mother and breaking the rules laid down by his religion he was not honest. There was one more event of the same kind. Once when fifteen years of age he stole a small piece of gold from his older brother, and the deed lay heavy on his mind. Finally he wrote out the story of what he had done, asking that he be punished and promising that he never again would steal. Feeling very much ashamed, he gave this letter to his good father, then a sick man. The father read it carefully, closed his eyes in thought, and the tears came. He slowly tore up the letter. The boy had expected angry words, and the sorrowful but loving feelings of the father were never to be forgotten by the son.

In England

At the age of eighteen Gandhi went to a college, but remained for only part of the year. The lessons did not interest him and he did not do well. Soon after this he was advised to go to England to study to be a lawyer. This would not be easy. It was difficult for him to leave India and to go to a foreign land where he would have to eat and drink with foreigners. This was against his religion, and most leaders of his group were against his going. Yet, in spite of all difficulties, the young Mohandas, at the age of eighteen, sailed for England, leaving a wife and child behind.

On board ship he wore, for the first time, the new foreign clothes provided by his friends. He wore his black suit, carefully keeping his new white clothes until he reached England. This was at the end of autumn, and on landing he was much troubled to find he was the only person so dressed. To make matters worse, he could not get at his baggage to change his clothes. In his own account of his early days in London, we find two interesting events.

One of these was his difficulty in finding suitable food. Unlike most of the Indians in England, he followed the rule of his religion and would not eat meat. This was not easy, and he was often hungry at the end of a meal. What was his joy when he discovered a dining-place where no meat of any sort was served. He learned for the first time that there were many people in England who for health reasons ate no meat. It pleased him to find science giving support to his religious beliefs. Later he found it easier to prepare breakfasts and suppers in his own room, and to buy his meals in the middle of the day.

The other event is one which later gave him and his friends much amusement. The young Indian tried to "play the English gentleman". He decided that if he could not eat like an Englishman, he would dress like one and act like one in other ways. He bought new clothes and a tall silk hat, and asked his brother to send him a gold watch-chain. Then he spent some time each morning dressing with care and brushing his thick hair. Following the advice of friends, he took lessons in dancing, French, playing a musical instrument and speaking in public. But in these arts he did not do very well, and his money was rapidly disappearing. At the end of three months he saw that he was not making the best use of his time, and gave up all this. He began to study law.

At this time also he became more interested in religions. When friends asked him to help them in their understanding of the Gita, the holy book of his own Hindu religion, he began to see how beautiful it was. Before long it became for him the one book for the best knowledge of Truth. Someone gave him a Bible, and in it he found some teachings of Jesus which he liked very much because they were so like certain ideas in the Gita. Then from a reading of a book by the English writer Carlyle, he learned about the Prophet Muhammad and about his greatness and bravery and simple living. At this time he was beginning to learn that the truth he loved was not to be found in any one religion only.

India Again

After four years of study, young Gandhi passed his law examinations and in 1891 returned to India. When he landed he was met by friends who told him of his mother's death. This was an even greater shock to him than the death of his father before he went to England. The next few years were not happy ones. He found his work as a lawyer not at all interesting, and came to feel that he was not fitted for this kind of occupation. He had trouble on the one occasion when he was in court. He almost fainted, and when his turn came to speak he could not say a word. He would welcome a change. This came when he was invited to go to South Africa to advise a rich Indian merchant who was trying to collect a large amount of money from a member of his family. We find him at the age of twenty-four in Durban, South Africa.

In South Africa

Gandhi soon found that conditions among the many Indians in South Africa were not at all right. He learned this first when he went to court wearing foreign clothes and a turban. The judge of the court ordered him to take off his turban. He refused and left the court. This turban was soon to become famous all over South Africa. Most of the Indians who had left their own land to look for work in Africa were considered of a low rank and were known as "coolies". Gandhi was thus a "coolie" lawyer.

A few days after he arrived, Gandhi was sent off to another city on business for his employer, Abdullah Sheth. When a white man travelling in the same train discovered him in a first-class seat he called a railway guard who ordered him to leave the first-class carriage. Gandhi replied that he had bought a first-class ticket and intended to use it. A policeman came and forced him to leave the train. The next day something even worse happened. While making a journey in a large public carriage, he was given a seat outside with the driver. During the journey the white man in charge wanted his seat. When Gandhi refused to move, the man struck him, but the other white people in the carriage made the man stop. When he reached the city he drove to the main hotel, and there received another shock. The hotel would not take him in. It was events like these which made Gandhi feel that someone was needed to help the Indians in Africa. He himself was not proud, and he was not dependent upon a comfortable way of living. Later he accepted for himself the simple living of the poorest Indians, and travelled third-class in trains at all times. But it hurt him to see the people of his country treated badly, and so he continued to work against all attempts to treat him and others in a way that was not fair and just.

After a time he came to feel that it would be unwise for the merchant who employed him to go to the courts to get back the money that was owed him. As a result of very hard work lasting months, he was able to get the two merchants to agree outside of court upon the amount of money to be paid and how it was to be paid. This success led him to believe that most quarrels between people could be, and should be, settled in a peaceful manner with the aid of friends.

During this year he met a number of Christians who were eager that he should become a Christian and Moslems who hoped that he would become a Moslem. He read from the Bible and Koran and from books about both religions. But at the same time he was coming to enjoy and depend more and more upon the holy books of Hinduism, and was coming to find for himself deep happiness and peace in them.

At the end of a year his work with Abdullah Sheth was finished and he planned to return to India. But at a goodbye dinner given him in Durban he learned that a law was being planned to take away from all Indians still more of their rights. During the talk at the dinner it was decided that Gandhi must remain in South Africa and work for the rights of the Indians. Thus began twenty years of hard work for the Indians of South Africa.

His Life-work Begins

At the end of three years he returned to India for several months, and then came back by ship with his wife and two children. While in India he had tried to tell the people there how Indians were treated in South Africa, and news of what he had spoken and written had reached the white people living in Natal before he arrived. When he attempted to land he was recognized, and cries of "Gandhi, Gandhi!" quickly brought a crowd together. The crowd gathered around him, threw stones and eggs at him and struck him. He was saved by the courage of the wife of the English

Chief of Police, who walked along with him until policemen came to his help. He was then able to escape from the angry crowd by dressing himself as an Indian policeman and slipping out of the back door while the Police Chief held the crowd's attention in front.

It is not possible to describe all the events of the years that Gandhi spent in South Africa serving his fellow Indians, and working to improve their conditions and to make the government treat them more justly. He gave up a position in which he was earning a lot of money in order to join with the poor people for whom he was working. In all his work his wife helped him, and believed in him and gave him courage to go on. From the struggle in South Africa he gained a strong belief in certain ways of action which were to be so important later in his own country. More and more he came to believe in a "soul force". This was a struggle against evil and force, not by using hatred and force, but by love and by quietly refusing to obey unjust laws. Those who believed as he did and followed him would not work with the government or obey an unjust law. In the end there was little that the government could do about it. Gandhi was often put in prison, but his followers continued to carry on the work. When Gandhi left South Africa in 1914 very great improvements in the conditions of the Indians there had taken place.

India and Work for the Poor

Gandhi returned to India at the beginning of the First World War to find himself already recognized as a leader. His work in South Africa had been followed by the people, and he now was everywhere spoken of as "Mahatma" Gandhi. He settled down near Ahmedabad, where he started an Ashram, a religious group-home. People of any race or religion were invited to come and join him, if they were willing to make certain promises. These were: (1) always to speak the truth; (2) not to fight or hate other people; (3) to eat only what was necessary to keep them healthy; (4) not to own anything that was not necessary.

The Untouchables were the lowest rank in the Hindu religion; they were allowed to do only the lowest kind of work; but they were welcome in the Gandhi home. When a family of Untouchables did come to join the group trouble arose. The neighbours threatened that they would have nothing to do with them, and the rich Hindus who were helping to support the home with money suddenly stopped giving. Gandhi was not troubled, but started making plans to move the whole group into the part of the city where the Untouchables lived. He planned that they all would get their living by doing the low work that only Untouchables were allowed to do. While these plans were being made, the Mahatma was called aside by a Moslem merchant, who asked him if he would accept money from him for the help of the Ashram. The next day the man returned with a large amount of money, enough to keep the home going for a year. Gandhi said: "God has sent us help at the last moment." This event was the first of many which was to give the Untouchables a new place in Indian life. At this time, and for the rest of his life, the Mahatma was wearing the simple native clothing made of cotton cloth spun in a home.

Gandhi's great aim in life was to help to improve the conditions of poor and suffering people, and to aid his people in any way he could, but always without using force. He was against every sort of evil, no matter of what kind. When he tried to find out about the conditions among poor farm workers, the people crowded around him by the hundreds. A friend had come among them, someone who wanted to help them, and to them this was something new. When the police ordered Gandhi to leave the place, he refused, and in court he explained why he could not obey. Then he asked the court to punish him for breaking the law. The court did not know what to do with such a man, and so let him go free. This was the first step in what came to be an important and common event in many parts of India—to refuse to obey a law considered to be unjust, and at the same time calmly to accept any punishment that might be given.

The March to the Sea

Little by little the people of India came to understand what the Mahatma meant by fighting force with love, instead of fighting force with force. In 1930 there was the famous Salt March.

According to the law, no one was allowed to make salt from sea water, but must buy it through the government.

Gandhi at the end of a day's march

Gandhi considered that this was a bad and unjust law and so should not be obeyed. He said publicly that he would lead his followers to the sea, two hundred miles away, and there disobey the law. For three weeks, while the whole world watched and while conditions in India were troubled, the little old man, dressed in the white cotton which he had spun himself, walked steadily on. Crowds followed him, the people changing from village to village, on and on, until they reached the sea. There he made a handful of salt. God had given the sea; no government of man could keep it from the people. He was put in prison for a time, but not for long.

Self-government for India

The struggle of the Indian people for self-government had begun. Gandhi wanted self-government, but he knew that Indians must show that they were ready for it. "Even God," he said, "cannot grant it; we must work for it and win it ourselves." He began to attack the British government in his writings because it was unwilling to free India, but he still believed in love and not hatred, and he set his face against the use of force. He was sent to prison several times because of what he said and what he did. When his followers did not obey him and used force, he went without food, sometimes for so long that he almost died.

His followers grew in number and in strength. Crowds gathered to see him pass and to hear him speak. All India read what he wrote. Important leaders of India and other parts of the world came to talk with him about their plans, and to listen to his message of peace and love for the world. The struggle for self-government was long, and in the end success came. After long years an Act was passed making India a free nation. Everyone knew that the man who had done more than anyone else to bring this about was Gandhi. But Gandhi was troubled in spite of his success. Such terrible quarrels had arisen between the Moslems and the

Hindus that India had had to be divided between them, and there were now two countries: India for the Hindus and Pakistan for the Moslems. Gandhi so loved his country and so hated quarrels that this division made him very unhappy.

The End Draws Near

Terrible things happened in many parts of India, especially where Hindus and Moslems lived side by side. Fighting between the two groups broke out, and men, women and children were killed. Hundreds of thousands of people were without homes and there was very great suffering. In the part of the country in which Gandhi was living, peace came sooner than in other parts of India, because Gandhi had said that he would refuse to eat until the fighting stopped. Both Hindus and Moslems respected him so much that they kept the peace. But Gandhi's life was coming to its end. On January 30, 1948, he was walking slowly from his home to attend a prayer meeting. A young Hindu thought that Gandhi had done harm to the Hindus because he was friendly with the Moslems; he pushed his way through the crowd and shot Gandhi in the stomach. Some minutes later a man came out of the house into which the body had been carried and said to the waiting crowd: "Gandhi is dead!"

Another great Indian leader, Pandit Nehru, speaking over the radio that night, said: "The light has gone out of our lives and everywhere it is dark. The father of the nation is no more. The best prayer we can offer is to give ourselves to Truth, and carry on the noble work for which he lived and for which he died." A few days later, following the custom of the Hindu religion, Mahatma Gandhi's body was burned in the presence of a great crowd, and later the ashes were scattered over the waters of the sacred rivers. So ended the life, but not the spirit, of one of the great men of the world.

Two

FLORENCE NIGHTINGALE

HAVE you ever been sick and cared for in a hospital? Or have you ever visited sick friends in a hospital? If so, then you probably have noticed how clean everything is and how quiet and how well arranged. Nurses dressed in white move about from bed to bed, carrying out the orders of the doctors and caring for the sick. These hard-working women are usually very calm and friendly and cheerful, doing all they can to make the life of the sick people more comfortable and as free from pain as they can. One leaves a hospital with a feeling of gratefulness for the cleverness of the doctors and for the loving care of the nurses.

But hospitals were not always like this. Nurses were not always clean and cheerful and helpful. In fact, not so many years ago things were quite different and people were afraid to enter a hospital. The person who helped to make these changes, more than any person in all the world, was Florence Nightingale, often called "The Lady of the Lamp".

Early Life

In the year 1820 Mr. and Mrs. Nightingale, the father and mother of Florence, were travelling in Europe. They settled down in the city of Florence, Italy. Here a daughter was born to them, whom they at once called Florence, after the Italian city. Already there was a daughter, aged two, who had been named Parthenope, or Parthe, after the Greek name for the city of Naples, Italy, where she had been born. After the birth of Florence, the family returned to their home in England.

Florence Nightingale

Mr and Mrs Nightingale were fine people, but they were not very well suited to each other. The mother was pretty, gay, rather selfish and loved pleasure. The father was pleasant and kind, but rather lazy. He was content to spend his days in hunting and fishing, reading and travel, and he had enough money to be able to live without serious work.

As little Florence grew up, she was not a happy child. If she had been a bad girl, her mother would have understood her. But she was not bad—she was different, strange, unhappy. Her home-life was pleasant enough, and the two little girls had their horses, dogs, cats and birds to play with. But Florence had a feeling that she was different from other children, and that the pleasant life of her home was not the kind of life which she wanted. She had a great deal of imagination and escaped into a dream world. She told stories to herself, stories in which she played the chief part. She did not feel at all close in spirit to her mother.

Most of the teaching of the two girls was done by their father and by a lady teacher who came to the house. But although the father was a good teacher the plan brought difficulties. Sister Parthe was not much interested in the long, hard lessons in history and language which the father gave them. So more and more Florence became the companion of her father in the library, and Parthe the companion of her mother in the living-room. This division in the family increased as time went on, and the results were not pleasant.

It is possible for us today to know much about Florence Nightingale's inner feelings because all her life she used to write down her thoughts and her feelings. At this time especially, she was unhappy, and with no close friends to talk to she poured out her thoughts on paper. She wrote on all sorts of paper—little pieces, big pieces, torn pieces. A large number of these have been kept and can be read today.

Voices

At this time in her life something very important happened to her. It seems not to be far different in many ways from what happened to the little French girl, Joan of Arc. In one of Florence's writings we read the following: "On February 7, 1837, God spoke to me and called me to His service." This was not merely a dream, for she declares that she heard a voice outside herself, speaking aloud in words.

She was then not quite seventeen years of age, and at times was living in a kind of dream world. But nearly forty years later she wrote that during her life "voices" had spoken to her at four different times.

But the voice did not make it clear to her what she was to do. She knew that God had called her to his service, but what this was she did not yet know. The idea of nursing did not come to her mind. She doctored her dolls; she cared for her animals; she liked babies. That was all. But she was at peace, and felt certain that one day God would speak again.

First Plans

A number of years were to pass before the way became clear. And these years were most difficult ones. For a time she travelled in Europe; she was gay in London. Then came illness, and unhappiness and misunderstandings with her sister and her mother. There were two events which helped her to believe that her life-work was to be with hospitals and the care of the sick. Her grandmother fell sick, and she was allowed to take care of her. She also cared for an old woman who had long served the family and who was ill for a time. Then she was allowed to nurse the sick among the poor people of the village in which they lived. But out of this service she learned one important thing. It was commonly believed that to be a good nurse one had only to be a woman and to be kind and helpful. Florence came to believe that a nurse must be trained, and know what to do and when and how to do it. But how and where could she possibly get this necessary training for herself?

Suddenly she had an idea. Not too far from her home there was a hospital, and the head doctor of the hospital was a family friend. What could be better? She would ask her family to let her work there for three months. She told her family of the plan. And then the storm broke. Her father was very much displeased. Was it for this that he had taught his daughter so many things, and taken her around Europe and bought her pretty clothes in Paris? The mother was frightened, then very angry and then burst into tears. Poor Florence! No one was on her side; she was lost; her courage was gone. She wrote at this time: "I can see no reason for living on. I shall never do anything, and am worse than dust and nothing."

Hospitals in the Past

As we see this young woman of twenty-five struggling to find her place in life, it is very easy to blame the father and mother, but it is perhaps not fair to judge them too hastily. In 1845 hospitals were terrible places—dirty, crowded, badly arranged, full of smells and disorder. Fifty or sixty beds were crowded together in large rooms, with only two feet of space between beds. In winter the rooms were heated by a single fireplace placed at one end. Windows were kept closed. The sick were for the most part poor creatures from the poor parts of the city. They came in dirty, they remained dirty, they left (if they were still alive) dirty. They drank and fought, and often the police were called in to bring order.

But the real reason why her family and friends did not want her to work in a hospital was the nurses. For the most part the nurses were not trained, and they were not good women at all. In fact, they were just the opposite—they were women of bad character. They used strong drink and became drunk. The head nurse of one large hospital told Florence that in her many years of service she had never known a nurse who did not drink heavily.

Eight years had now passed since her "call", and eight more years were to pass before she was free to follow her desires. These last eight years were the hardest, and it is only because she was so determined that she kept on. She refused to marry a man whom she loved when he wanted her to marry him, and it caused her sorrow. But how could she marry and yet carry out the work to which she had been called? She was very much interested in hospitals. She read all she could find about hospitals. She looked at reports about hospitals, learned of the number of sick people and the kinds of diseases they had. She worked in the early hours of cold mornings to increase her knowledge of hospital conditions; then she joined her family in the usual life of their home.

Her Life Plans Begin

There was one happy time when, without the permission of her father and mother, she worked, and oh so hard, in a hospital in Germany. But at home there were illnesses and sorrows and misunderstandings. And yet, all the time she was growing in strength of mind and character and gaining valuable knowledge, and the days of freedom were not far off.

In the spring of 1853 she was invited to take charge of a nursing-home for ladies who could no longer pay for hospital care. The group of people in charge was planning to move the home to another place and needed a person who would be able to act as head. Against the wishes of her family, Florence agreed to take the position with the understanding that she was to receive no pay for her work. But she was to have the power to get things done. At this time her father agreed to give her for her own use five hundred English pounds each year; so the money arrangements with the hospital made no difference to her. She at once took up her new work. In a short time she was doing a thousand things, from caring for the ill to arranging for the placing of sick-room bells, and the examination of medicines, food, bed-making and coal for the fires. It was hard work, but it was satisfying work and she enjoyed it.

At this time she is described as being tall, graceful and pleasant, with a sweet smile and a friendly manner. The sick ladies liked her very much, as shown in their letters to her: "My dearest kind Miss Nightingale, I send you a few lines of love." "Thank you . . . you are our sunshine . . . were you to give up, all would soon fade away." But beneath the friendliness and sweetness there was a will of steel. She knew how to make people work together and how to arrange the work in the best way.

All that Florence Nightingale had done up to this time seemed but to be in preparation for what was to come. Great events were about to take place, events in which she was to play an important part.

Beginning of the Crimean War

War had broken out between England and Russia, and a British army had been sent to destroy the Russian army in the Crimea on the Black Sea. The British army was directed from Scutari, a large village near Constantinople. The soldiers fought bravely enough, but they had not proper tents, or food, or doctors' care. When thousands were wounded they could not be cared for; many suffered terribly and died. When thousands became sick with a disease which spread among them, they were not cared for. Thousands suffered and died. The wounded and the sick lay in long lines on the floor, without food or water or care.

Suffering among soldiers was nothing new; it was well known in the army. But the people of England had never known about it. No one had told them. Now, for the first time, a newspaper writer from one of the important London newspapers visited the battle-fields, the camps, the hospitals. And he wrote what he had seen, and his paper in London printed the terrible stories. There were stories of wounded men who were forced to wait a week before a doctor looked at their wounds; of wounds that could not be cared for because there were no bandages and no one to put on the bandages.

When the articles appeared in the London paper, the people of England were terribly angry. They demanded that something be done. Why were there not enough doctors and nurses and supplies? Whose fault was it? One of the men who was blamed was Sidney Herbert, who held an important government position. He was a good friend of Florence Nightingale, and knew about her work and her knowledge of hospitals. In a letter to her he expressed his thoughts in words that were not greatly different from the following:

The Call Comes

"Women nurses are needed in the hospital in Scutari for I am sure the poor wounded are now treated very roughly. . . . A number of ladies have offered to go out, but they have no idea what a hospital is like nor what their duties would be. . . . There is but one person in England that I know of who would be able to choose nurses and go out to do the work that needs to be done. . . . The task is a very difficult one. . . . Will you accept it? . . . I know you will decide wisely. . . . God grant that your answer may be yes. . . ."

Miss Nightingale was ready and eager to go. She was especially eager to prove the value and importance of nurses. The eyes of the nation were on Scutari. If women nurses were able to be of service to the sick and wounded under the difficult conditions which were found in Scutari, then never again would nurses and nursing be looked down upon. This was a golden chance to prove their worth, and she welcomed it. But first nurses must be found . . . how? and where? This was not an easy task and time was short, but soon thirty-eight women, more or less suitable, were found. No young women were chosen; only a few had had real training; most were going because they were paid more than they could get in England. Special clothes were hastily made for them. They were grey in colour and not pretty, and didn't fit very well, but at least "Miss Nightingale's nurses" had one thing in common.

Turkey

The days of preparation were few and very busy. Now, with Florence chosen by the government to do such important work, Mrs Nightingale and sister Parthe were more friendly, and hurried to London to help her. The party of nurses crossed over to France, went by train to the south of France, and from there took a ship to Constantinople. The sea voyage was very stormy, and poor Florence spent all the time in bed, seasick. But at last, on November 3, 1854, they reached Constantinople and went on shore. With a cold wind blowing, hungry dogs fighting, a dead horse floating in the water, a few wounded men standing about, the group of nurses climbed up the slope to the gigantic hospital.

Hospital Conditions

From a distance the great building, built for Turkish soldiers and now used as a hospital, looked like a splendid giant's palace. But inside, how different! Built around a courtyard, in the form of a square, were miles of rooms and halls, with broken floors and wet walls. One part had been burned and was no longer used. In one part of the building was a camp for soldiers; in another were rooms where horses were kept; a third part was used as a wine-shop. And to make matters worse the drinking water had been shut off and the waste pipes were stopped up. More of the wounded brought into the building died from diseases caught in the building than died from their wounds.

There was disorder everywhere, and no one person seemed to be in charge. Soon it would be winter, and already the hospital was without supplies that a hospital needs. Even such supplies as knives and forks and spoons and shirts could not be given the soldiers. And why? The army rules said that when a soldier came to a hospital he should bring with him his bag containing his clothes and other things which the army had given him. But how could they bring them? Their own had been thrown away or left behind in the disorder of battle, by men who were glad to escape with their lives. But the men in charge of these supplies, even when they had them on hand, refused to give them out. "Sorry, my good fellow," they said, "you should have kept your own. These are army rules." A silly rule? Yes, and very, very cruel.

Unwelcome

Miss Nightingale and her party of thirty-eight nurses were given a few rooms which had been occupied by three doctors. The rooms were very small and dirty, and there was nothing in them except rats, insects, three chairs and the body of a dead Russian officer. The doctors in the hospital were not happy to see the nurses arrive because they did not want them there. Who were these nurses? And what could a group of women do in a hospital for soldiers? The doctors decided to pay no attention to them. And Miss Nightingale, for her part, was determined that the nurses must not work in the hospital unless they were invited to do so by the doctors. Nurses must help the doctors and carry out their orders. It would be unwise for them to attempt to work alone. She knew that they must wait to be asked. And wait they did. For almost a week they sat around, making bandages, waiting, while the sick lay around uncared for.

The first chance to help was with the food in the kitchens, where conditions were terrible. The careless cooks used to place large pieces of meat in pots of water and build fires under the pots. When they thought the meat was cooked enough, they ordered the helpers to put out the fires by throwing water on them. The pieces of meat, cooked or uncooked, were carelessly served to the sick of the hospital. Some of the sick received uncooked meat; some received mostly bones. Some got none; those who were very sick couldn't eat meat. "Never mind! Better luck next time!" There were seldom any vegetables to eat. And tea? Well, the tea was made in the unwashed pots in which the meat had just been cooked, and the taste was so bad that no one could drink it. Florence Nightingale was at last allowed to enter the kitchens, and to see that the sick had well-cooked and more suitable food. But this was all she was permitted to do at first.

Work Begins

And then came the big change. Conditions in the Crimea became worse and worse. The rain, the mud, the lack of food and shelter, the cold of the early winter—all working together brought serious trouble to the British army. The sick began to pour down from the Black Sea. Then, as if conditions were not already bad enough, a terrible windstorm swept across the sea. Buildings were destroyed, trees torn down, tents blown away, ships sunk, supplies ruined. The poor soldiers were left half buried in mud and icy water, with no covering, no food. Day by day the sick and tired-out men poured into the hospital until every room was filled and the halls as well. Men lay in lines on the floor everywhere. In the hospital all was upside-down and in disorder as the number of men increased.

The doctors, especially the older men, worked like lions, and were often on their feet for twenty-four hours at a time. But conditions were very bad. There were no bedclothes, not enough medicines and other supplies, and no one knew how to get them. The sick lay on the floors covered with dirt, and no one knew what to do about it. The work of this great hospital, crowded with thousands of wounded and sick and suffering and dying, was in complete disorder. In despair the doctors turned to Florence Nightingale and her nurses.

The group of nurses began work, helping wherever their help was needed. And little by little conditions began to improve. The busy doctors soon came to understand that there was one person in Scutari who had the money and the power and could get things done. Miss Nightingale had a large amount of money from London, which she could use and which she did use. The floors were terribly dirty—she bought two hundred brushes and quantities of rough cloth and the floors were made clean. The soldiers' clothes had not been washed for five weeks—she rented a house, hired washerwomen, and the clothes were made clean. Supplies of all kinds were missing—she sent to the markets of Constantinople and bought what was needed: knives and forks, scissors and combs, soap and tables, shirts and pots.

At the beginning of December word came that six hundred more sick and wounded were on their way from the Black Sea. The hospital was completely filled; there was no place to put them. Of course, if the burned part of the building which was now not used could only be repaired, that would take one thousand more men. But to repair it would take workmen and money, and there was no one to give the order to have it done. That is, no one except Miss Nightingale.

Florence in Charge

She took matters into her own hands, hired two hundred workmen and put them to work. When the sick and wounded arrived, not six hundred but eight hundred, their beds were ready. One of the sick men described how he felt when he got off the dirty boat which had brought them to Scutari, and was received by Miss Nightingale and the

A hospital ward at Scutari

nurses with a clean bed and warm food: "We felt we were in heaven," he said.

The relations between Miss Nightingale and her mixed group of nurses were not always happy. She felt it was necessary to have order and obedience within her group of nurses, because above all she wanted to prove to the world the value of women nurses. She knew that the presence of a few women working among thousands of men brought difficulties that made obedience to her orders necessary.

Some of the nurses complained about the ugly caps they were forced to wear. Some complained because they were forbidden to enter the sick-rooms after eight o'clock at night. Some complained because they were not allowed to give a sick soldier the simple, good food they knew he needed unless a doctor had ordered it. A few of the nurses disliked Miss Nightingale and felt that she was too firm and difficult to please. It took some time before they were willing cheerfully to follow the rules which she laid down.

At this time her life was very busy and difficult. Her health had never been very good, and the living conditions at Scutari were most undesirable. When it rained, water poured through the roof of her room. The food was almost uneatable. She seldom left the hospital building to go anywhere. When the sick came pouring in, she was sometimes on her feet for twenty-four hours. But always her manner with the men was gentle and kind. The men admired and loved her. She was able to make them stop using bad words in their talk, to stop drinking, and to get them to write home to their families. She gave them courage to let the doctor operate on them without complaint. The eyes of the sick followed her as she passed through the sick-rooms at night, her lamp in her hand. "What a comfort it was even to see her pass," wrote one soldier. "She would speak to one, smile to as many more; but she could not do it all, you know. We lay there by the hundreds; but we could kiss her shadow as it fell and lay our heads down . . . again content."

Visit to the Crimea

When spring-time came and conditions in the hospital were much better, she went up to the Crimea, to Balaclava, to visit the hospital there. But the examination was short. She came down with a high fever, the Crimean fever, and was seriously ill. For two weeks she lay between life and death. The soldiers at Balaclava were sad. In the hospital at Scutari when the men heard the news, they turned their faces to the wall and wept. All their trust was in her. In England the news of her illness was received with great sorrow, and when word came that she was getting better strangers stopped one another in the streets to tell the good news. When she was able to be moved, she returned to Scutari, and after a few weeks she was back in the hospital again.

Miss Nightingale's work at this time fell into two parts. The first was during the terrible winter of 1854–5, when she was in charge of the hospital and soon received the support of all. The second was from the spring to her return to England in the summer of 1856.

Difficult Times

The second part was not a happy one. There were people in the hospital and in the army who became her enemies. When the people in England learned of the bad conditions among the common soldiers, they were angry. When they learned of the disorder in the hospitals and in the army, there was a storm of complaint. Some of the head doctors and officers did not like this and tried to blame Miss Nightingale. They spoke against her and her work, and wanted her to leave. It was not a pleasant time for her.

But she refused to give up. Indeed, she added another aim to her work. She was determined to improve the conditions among the common soldiers. Their officers sometimes treated them like mere animals. Miss Nightingale, who had come to know them well, believed they behaved in the way they did because they were given no chance to behave differently. "Give them a chance," she wrote to her sister Parthe, "to send money quickly and safely home and they will use it. Give them schools and interesting talks and they will come to them. Give them books and games and amusements and they will stop drinking. Give them suffering and they will bear it. Give them work and they will do it."

Helping the Soldiers

She felt that she must look after the soldiers, not only when they were ill but when they were well. What she did for them outside the hospital was as important as what she did inside the hospital. Although many of the army officers did not like it, she opened a small reading-room for men who were able to walk but not leave the hospital. Their behaviour was excellent. But when she wanted to hire a teacher to teach those who could not read or write, she was refused. "You are spoiling them," she was told.

She found that the men spent their small pay on drink because it was not easy to send money to their families. She therefore made a custom of spending one afternoon a week in her room, and the money brought to her by the men was quickly and safely sent on to England.

Then a reading-room was opened and furnished with tables and chairs, with maps and pictures on the walls. From her own money she bought paper, pens and ink and newspapers. Here the men sat quietly, reading and writing. They crowded the halls to hear interesting talks. Groups came to singing classes. The men themselves made a little theatre and acted plays. Football was played by those who were well; quieter games were played by the sick. It is largely because of the work of Florence Nightingale that the picture of the common soldier as a drunken beast disappeared, never to return.

This was a busy time, with its happy sides and also its unpleasant sides. But in April peace came between the two countries, Russia and England, and the work in the hospital became lighter. In July the last sick soldier left the Scutari hospital and her task was ended. She could go home.

Back Home

But even going home was not an easy matter, for all England wished to honour her. The attacks of her enemies could never stand against the praises of the many whom she had served. During the months of the war, wounded and sick by the thousands had written home about her and her loving care. So now in England plans were being made to welcome her home. There were to be crowds of cheering people, music, speeches and gifts. They wanted to show her what they thought of her and her work. The government wished to send her home on a warship. But she wanted none of all this. She went on a regular ship, travelling under the name of "Miss Smith", to southern France. Then across France by train, by boat to England, then on to London and home. Her father, mother and sister were sitting quietly together when she arrived. The old servant, sitting in her own room in the front of the house, was the first to see her. She looked up, saw a lady in black walking alone up the path. She looked again, gave a loud cry, burst into tears and rushed out to meet her. Florence Nightingale had returned.

After the War

She was home, and she was tired out and ill. But there was much work to be done. She was determined to fight to bring about better conditions among the common soldiers in the army, for she had seen the conditions and knew how bad they were. But she felt that she must first gain the respect of those in power in England. She felt that these people would never respect her, or listen to her, so long as the public praised her and looked upon her as someone in a story-book. They would dislike her and would not believe that such a woman had anything useful to offer. So she purposely set out to destroy her fame. That is why, after her return to England, she never appeared in public, never made a speech, never attended a party. She wanted the public to forget her, and she very nearly succeeded. Within a year most people, because they heard nothing more about her, believed that she was probably dead.

Most people who have heard of Florence Nightingale think only of her work in the hospital at Scutari during the Crimean War. That is only natural, for it was what she did there that made it possible to succeed in what came later. And yet, she was in Scutari for less than two years, and when she returned she was only thirty-six years old. Many, many years of service lay before her, and the things she was able to do in those years are so many that it would take a long book to describe them all.

Her Life Aims

There were times when she was ill and could not leave her bed for months and even years. There were times when she worked day and night, visiting hospitals, making plans for the care of the poor and the sick, talking with important government officers, writing reports. Two great aims were ever before her: improving the conditions of the common soldiers in the army, and making nursing a well-paid, respected life-work for women. In both of these aims she had great success, and the world is the richer for her long life of service.

Because of her, nursing is what it is today. The Nightingale Training School for Nurses was started near one of the large hospitals of England. The fine training that thousands of young women received here during the years that followed has greatly changed nursing all over the world. The little book on nursing which she wrote at this time is still interesting to read. It may contain little which is new to people today, but to the people of her day her ideas were most surprising. Thousands of copies were sent to mills, workshops, villages and schools, and it was translated into three European languages. The simple, direct advice on the care of sick people was much needed and most helpful.

Last Days

In her later years kings and queens honoured her; government officers and famous doctors came to her for advice about hospitals; nurses and the sick poor for whom she worked were grateful to her. But as the years went by she was able to do less and less. She died quietly in her own home at the age of ninety. On her grave is a stone, marked simply: F.N. Born 1820 . . . Died 1910.

Three

ABRAHAM LINCOLN

IT was in the early days of American life. A man was working in the fields near his log *cabin*, and close by were his three sons. Danger? Yes, of course there was always some danger, for in the thick forests there were Indians, some friendly and some unfriendly.

Indians!

Suddenly there was a shot and the father fell to the ground, dead. Indians! One of the boys started off at once to bring help from the nearest fort. The second boy hurried to the cabin to get his gun. Just as he seized his gun he looked back. An Indian was bending over to pick up and carry away the little six-year-old brother who had been left behind, beside the dead father. Quickly the boy aimed his gun and fired. The Indian fell forward on his face and lay still. The little boy then ran to join his older brother in the cabin, and the two were able to keep back the unfriendly Indians until help arrived from the fort. It was the little boy, Thomas, saved by the quick action of his brother, who was later to become the father of Abraham Lincoln.

Early American Life

Our story begins in the State of Kentucky, not many years after the American states had joined together to make a new nation—the United States. People coming from Europe had settled first in the eastern part of the country, along the Atlantic Ocean. Then the bolder among them had moved west, where there were wild animals and Indians,

Abraham Lincoln

mountains and valleys, great forests and wide plains. Some of the Indians welcomed the newcomers and helped them; others fought to keep them from coming. These brave settlers cut down trees, built log cabins and planted their crops. More and more people followed them; roads and villages and towns were built. Then the restless and bold among them left the towns and villages and moved still farther west into new land. This happened again and again, until slowly the whole country was settled.

As Tom Lincoln grew up he was unable to go to school, and at the time of his marriage he did not know how to read or write. His wife had studied a little, and she taught him to write his own name. In a rough log cabin on their farm near a small village in Kentucky two children were born to them. The first was a girl, Sarah, and then in 1809 there was a boy whom they named Abraham. The story is told that soon after the baby was born the young son of a neighbour was allowed to hold him in his arms for a few minutes. When little Abraham cried long and loud, the little boy called out: "Aunt, take him! He'll never come to much." By this he meant that in his opinion Abraham would never grow up to be worth much.

Home and School

As little Abraham grew older his only occupation was playing with his sister Sarah, and the forest was their playground. The house was one room, with one door and one window. When he was seven years old Abraham walked four miles a day to a little school-house. It was built of logs, with a dirt floor, a door and no windows. It must have been very noisy in the small room, for all the boys and girls learned their lessons by saying them aloud to themselves until it was time to say them to the teacher. The air was full of sounds: "A-B-C-D-E-F-G-. . . . Two and two make four. . . . School, s-c-h-o-o-l, school. . . . The fat cat ate the rat."

But Tom Lincoln was not satisfied with life in Kentucky. The soil of his farm was poor, and he dreamed of a better life farther to the west, where new lands had just been opened up. Little Abraham helped his father build a flat boat, and on it were heaped the goods from the house: tables and chairs and supplies. The father floated these down the river on the boat, while the mother and the two children went with the rest of the goods on two borrowed horses. They reached the new land. They had no horse, no cow, no house, and soon the winter storms would begin. There was no time to lose. Working together, they quickly cut down trees and built a simple cabin of logs, poles, dried branches and mud, open on one side. This would be all right until they could make something stronger and better.

The New Home

Though Abraham was only seven years old at this time, he was unusually large and strong for his age. He helped his father in all the hard work of cutting down the trees to make the cabin. From the age of seven to the age of twenty-three, the thing that he used most was an axe. Then came the making of the fields for the farm and the planting of the crops. The next year the new cabin was finished—one room eighteen feet square. It was simple: four walls with a roof, a dirt floor, no windows and a low door. A log fire gave light and heat to the room. Pieces of wood placed between the logs of one of the walls made a ladder leading to a floor in the upper part of the room. Here Abraham slept on a heap of leaves.

Their food was mostly the meat of wild animals which the father shot. They made clothes from the skins of the animals; they seldom wore shoes. The son had once killed a large bird by shooting through the crack in the logs, but it gave him an unpleasant feeling to kill animals. After this he seldom killed wild animals.

Sickness and Death

Unfortunately, with the coming of autumn there came sickness to the little group of people who had settled in that corner of the state. There was a common saying about the brave settlers and the many dangers of their life. It was: "The cowards never started and the weak ones died by the way." The nearest doctor was thirty miles away. Mrs Lincoln became ill and died. She was most certainly not one of the weak ones, but her strength was not great enough to fight against her serious illness. Her death was a cruel blow to the little family, especially as little Sarah was only eleven years old and too small to care for the home.

The next year Mr Lincoln was away from home for some time. When he returned he brought with him the new mother, a woman he had known for a long time. Her husband had died, leaving her with three children, two boys and a girl. She was a very fine woman and mother, and there was no difference in the way she treated the five children; she loved them all.

School and Books

Abraham grew to be big and strong and over six feet tall. He worked hard at all kinds of work because the family was always poor. If he was not working for his father, he was working for neighbours to get money for the family. But although he worked hard his heart was not in his work. The trouble was that he wanted very much to have more knowledge. At three different times in his life he was able to attend school for short times: when he was seven years old, and fourteen, and seventeen, making less than twelve months in all that he was in a schoolroom. But he was always asking questions, reading books, thinking. When he found something interesting he wrote it down, repeated it, learned it by heart. He spent long hours in the evening sitting in front of the open fire in the little cabin, studying and writing. As there was very little paper in the home, he used bits of burnt wood from the fire and wrote on a piece of wood. When the piece of wood was covered with black marks, he took his knife and cleaned it away.

One of the books he borrowed from a neighbour was *The Life of Washington*. Washington had been the first president of the United States, and was called the father of his country. Abraham liked the book so much that he took it up to bed with him, and put it between the cracks in the logs so that he could read it as soon as he woke up in the morning. Then one night it rained and water came through the cracks and damaged the book. The owner of the book made Lincoln work in his cornfield for three days to pay for the damage caused by the rain. However, this did not stop him from borrowing, and before long he had read every book owned by anyone living within fifty miles. He was hungry and thirsty to know more and more of what was hidden between the covers of books. He kept saying: "The things I want to know are in books; my best friend is the man who'll get me a book I haven't read."

He was kind and friendly and people liked him. His new mother once said of him: "I can say what hardly one mother in a thousand can say: Abe never gave me an unkind word or look, and never refused to do anything I asked him. . . . I must say that Abe was the best boy I ever saw or expect to see." Also, he could run faster, lift more and wrestle better than anyone else around. He was so strong that he could lift a weight of six hundred pounds. At eighteen he could hold a heavy axe in one hand, straight out from the shoulder and hold it steady. He walked thirty-four miles one day to hear a man make a speech, and enjoyed the walk and the speech.

Leaving Home

By the time Abraham, or Abe as he was often called, was twenty-one years of age there were many people living near them. The father felt that there were too many people. So the family moved again, this time to the State of Illinois. Here the young man stayed only long enough to help the family get settled in their new home. Then he left home to start life on his own, his axe on his shoulder and all his belongings in a pack in his hand. One of his first posts was helping to take a boat-load of goods down the river to New Orleans. First they had to build a flat boat. There were difficulties, but at last they got started, and in the end reached the big city port.

Slavery in New Orleans

It is probable that in New Orleans, during the month that he was there, the young Lincoln saw slavery in its worst form. It is probable also that what he saw of slavery helped to determine his later thinking and action. Over many years thousands of black people had been brought from Africa to the new world, and sold as slaves to work in the cotton-fields of the south. In the city newspapers Lincoln would read notices like the following:

For Sale: Several girls from 10 to 18 years old, a woman 24, a very valuable woman 25, with three clever children.

Wanted: I want to buy 25 black people, between the ages of 18 and 25, men and women, for which I will pay the highest prices.

While wandering around the city of New Orleans, Lincoln came to the slave-market, where slaves were being bought and sold. A young woman was being sold, and was looked at and talked about by the buyers as though she were a horse. The young Lincoln didn't like what he saw. In describing the scene later he said: "If I ever get a chance to hit this thing, I'll hit it hard."

When he returned to the north he was placed in charge of a store in a small town. He was more and more respected by the people in the town as they came to know him. If a poor woman needed wood for her fire, he cut it for her. If a cart was caught in the mud and couldn't move, he was the first to go to the aid of the driver. If he made a mistake in giving change to a buyer, he could not sleep until he had corrected the mistake, even though he had to walk miles into the country to do so. People depended on his kindness and his honesty, and thus he came to be known as "Honest Abe".

The Fight

In that part of the state there was a rough group of young men whose leader was a strong fellow named Jack Armstrong. The group loudly claimed that their leader was a better man than Lincoln and could easily beat him in wrestling. A merchant in the village was sure that Abe could win, and talked so much about it that the whole village became interested. Lincoln did his best not to be drawn into the fight, but agreed to fight when he saw that he would lose the respect of the village for being afraid. On the appointed day all the people of the village went out to the battle-field, very much excited to see which man would win. At this time Lincoln weighed about one hundred and eighty pounds and his arms were long and powerful.

Soon after the wrestling began it became certain to Armstrong's friends that their leader had met someone as strong and as clever as himself. In unfair ways they tried to give Jack help. This so angered Lincoln that he lifted Armstrong high in the air, shook him, and threw him heavily to the ground, flat on his back. For a few moments it seemed as though there would be trouble from Armstrong's followers. Lincoln stood with his back to a wall and invited them to come on, all of them. But Jack rose from the ground and pushed his way through the group. He seized Abraham by the hand and said, "The fight was a fair one. He is the best fellow who ever came to this settlement." After this, instead of being against Lincoln, the group became his friends and supporters. He was always welcome in their homes. Later on, as we shall see, Lincoln saved the life of Jack Armstrong's son.

Fighting Indians

In less than a year the man who owned the store closed it, and Lincoln was free to do as he pleased. He used this time to do more reading and studying with the teacher of the village school. This freedom also made it possible for him to join a group of men called by the governor of the State of Illinois to defend the state against the Indians. It was believed that unfriendly Indians were planning to try to get back land which they had earlier sold to the settlers. When this group of men met on the village square, they immediately chose Lincoln to be their captain. This honour came as a surprise to him, as he had been in the village for only a year. It gave him more pleasure than any of the many honours which came to him later. Fortunately the Indian attack was not serious, and after three months of rough living the men returned to their homes. Lincoln had seen no Indians at all, except one friendly Indian whom he had saved from some soldiers who had wanted to shoot him as a spy.

Abe the Store-keeper

Unfortunately, Abe's experiences as a store-keeper were not yet at an end. He and a man called Berry bought a store, and as they had very little money they had to borrow from others to pay for it. But the store was not a success. One reason for the failure to make money was that there were already too many stores in the small village, and another was that Lincoln was not clever at selling goods.

His heart was not in his work. Sometimes those who came to buy found him reading a book under a tree behind the store. Sometimes he weighed out sugar and flour for a buyer, still holding a book in one hand and eager to get back to his reading.

At the Bottom of the Barrel

Those who came to buy grew fewer and fewer in number. This gave Abe more time in which to read and study, but it did not help business. One day a settler on his way to the West stopped at the store. He had an old barrel which he wanted to sell. Abe didn't want the barrel, but to please the man he gave him something for it, about half a dollar, and the man drove on. Later, when he came to throw out the old paper in the bottom of the barrel he found a book. To his surprise and joy it was a famous book on law, a book that was owned by every lawyer. The book seemed to say: "Take me and read me; you were born to be a lawyer." He did read it.

Then one day Lincoln woke up to find that Berry had gone, leaving him with the many promises to pay which they had made to the people from whom they had borrowed the money to buy the store. Of course he could run away as Berry had done, and as so many others did, or he could try to pay back the borrowed money. For "Honest Abe" there was no choice. He told all the people to whom the promises had been made that he would pay back every dollar if they would give him time to get the money. From then on, all the money that he could spare went to paying back what had been borrowed. It took him seventeen years, seventeen long years; but the money was paid.

Abe the Law-maker

The years that followed were difficult and busy ones for Lincoln. Little by little his neighbours were coming to know him and like him. Perhaps one reason why he was elected to the government of the state at this time was because he had the support of many of the farmers. They liked a man who could talk to them about his ideas and the government, and at the same time work beside them in their fields. When he was elected the first time, he went to a friend and asked him: "Did you help elect me?" When the man answered that he had, Lincoln continued: "Good! I want to buy some clothes and dress a little better; I want to borrow two hundred dollars." Because he was young and inexperienced, he did not try to be a leader. He worked quietly, won the respect of the other makers of the laws, and gained much from the years spent there.

His election in 1834 marks the end of the first part of his life. He was finished now with the life of a settler, with rough companions and with careless living. He continued for many years to be a poor man, and sometimes he had no money at all. But from now on his life was to be spent with people with wider knowledge and larger ideas. During the eight years that he spent as an elected member of the government he was studying law, and at the end of that time he went to Springfield, Illinois. There he joined with an older man to practise law. He was then twenty-nine years old. He had only seven dollars in his pocket, not enough to rent a room by himself. But he faced the future hopefully.

Abe the Lawyer

For the next twenty-five years Lincoln worked hard as a lawyer. Before long he was known as a lawyer who was honest, who always spoke the truth and who always did what he thought was right. When two people quarrelled and wanted to go to the courts, Lincoln often talked with them and tried to get them to settle the matter between themselves without going to the courts. If he believed that a man was wrong he would not be his lawyer. He would never ask a person to pay more than was fair for what he had done for him. It is said that when people talked about Lincoln it was nearly always about one of the following things: (1) How tall, strong, quick and ugly-looking he was; (2) how well he told funny stories, and how pleasant and kindly he was; (3) how sad and silent he could be at times; (4) how he was always looking for the chance to learn something new; (5) how he was always ready to help a friend, or a stranger, or an animal.

In those days the judge of a court often travelled from one town to another to hold his court. The lawyers, Lincoln among them, followed along with him. Little by little, as people came to know and trust him, his law work grew.

Saving a Life

There came a day when Lincoln left everything and went to the help of Jack Armstrong's wife. Jack had died shortly before, and now his son Duff was in serious trouble. It was said that Duff had killed a man and that he should be punished by being put to death. One night Duff and another man had been drinking heavily. They had quarrelled and fought, and Duff knocked the other man down with a blow on the head. Five days later the man died.

Abe wanted very much to free the son of his old friend, if he could. He had known the family for years, and although he believed that Duff was rather wild, he did not believe that he was bad or that he had killed the man. A house-painter by the name of Allen claimed to have seen the fight between Armstrong and the other, and seen him strike the cruel blow.

"What time was it?" Allen was asked.

"Between ten and eleven at night," was the answer.

"And how could you see so clearly at that time of night?"

"By the moonlight."

"Was there enough light to see everything that happened?"

"The moon was about in the same place the sun would be at ten o'clock in the morning and nearly full," was the answer.

Lincoln then brought into the court a book which showed that on the night of the fight the moon had set just before midnight. At eleven o'clock the moon must have been low in the sky. There could have been very little light, and so it was doubtful if Allen could have seen what he claimed to see. As he had lied about the position of the moon, was it not probable that he had lied about the blow? Then came the time for Lincoln to address the twelve men who were to free Duff or have him put to death. He told them about the Armstrong family and how kind they had been to him. He said that they had made mistakes, like everyone else, but that they were good people. Certainly a man like Duff should not be put to death for something which he did not do. Duff was set free. Lincoln's last words to him were good advice: "Duff, go home and be a good boy now, and don't get into any more trouble."

The Question of Slavery

Although during these years Abraham Lincoln's work was that of a lawyer, he had not given up his interest in government. In fact, his interest was growing. He was especially interested in the question of slavery in the growing United States. More and more people were moving into the empty West and settling down in towns and villages. From these newly settled lands new states were formed and became part of the new nation . . . the United States. Slavery was permitted in the Southern states; it was not permitted in the Northern states. But what about slavery in these new states in the West? Should slavery be permitted there? Some people said yes; some people said no. Some said that the people who lived in these states should decide whether or not to have slavery; some said it should not be permitted north of a line drawn from the Atlantic to the

Pacific Ocean. It was a very difficult question and a very important one.

One of the great leaders of that time was Stephen Douglas. He was a very keen and able man, a powerful speaker, and greatly admired by the crowds. He wanted to be President of the United States, and tried to please the people of both the South and the North, and succeeded in the end by pleasing neither.

Lincoln did not believe that the slaves should suddenly be set free. But he did believe that slavery was wrong, and he did not want to see it spread to the other states, as he feared it might. "When the white man governs himself," he said, "that is self-government; but when he governs himself and also governs another man, that is more than self-government . . . that is despotism. . . . No man is good enough to govern another man without the other's consent." The battle for freedom had begun, and he was determined that he would not draw back. "I know there is a God," he said to a friend, "and He hates injustice and slavery. I see the storm coming. I know His hand is in it. If He has a place for me and work for me . . . and I think He has . . . I believe I am ready. I am nothing, but truth is everything."

Lincoln and Douglas

Lincoln and Douglas travelled about the State of Illinois and spoke at the same meetings to thousands of people. Each man gave his ideas about slavery and what the government and the courts ought to do. Both men were good speakers, for now Lincoln had learned to speak simply and with power. The great crowds were excited by their words, some praising the ideas of Douglas and some the ideas of Lincoln. It was these speeches, perhaps more than any other one thing, which caused Lincoln to be so widely known and so greatly respected. And yet the result of the elections of 1860 was a great surprise to him, and to his friends and to almost everyone. Abraham Lincoln, only a few years before an unknown, simple country lawyer, was chosen to be President of the United States.

In the White House

On February 11, 1861, he left Springfield, together with his wife and three small boys, on his journey to Washington and his new work in the White House. Before the train started on the long journey, he stood at the back of the last carriage and spoke to the many friends and neighbours who had come to say good-bye. He took off his tall, black hat, and stood looking at them for a moment, with tears in his eyes. These are some of his words: "My friends . . . to this place and the kindness of these people I owe everything. Here I have lived . . . and have passed from a young to an old man. Here my children have been born, and one is buried. I now leave, not knowing when or whether I may ever return, with a task before me greater than that which rested upon Washington. Trusting in Him, who can go with me, and remain with you, and be everywhere for good, let us . . . hope that all will yet be well. . . ."

Trusting in God and knowing very well that he faced a difficult task, Lincoln took up his duties as President of the United States. It was indeed a difficult time. Seven of the Southern states had already left the Union, displeased with the Northern ideas about slavery. They had set up a government of their own and had chosen a president. In the Northern states there was uncertainty and disorder. To permit these Southern states to leave the Union might destroy the nation, but how could one stop them? It was for President Lincoln to provide the answer. And he was inexperienced, with some advisers who were very weak, and one who felt himself to be so able that he wished the President to leave everything to him.

The Civil War Begins

Events followed one another rapidly. At Fort Sumter in the South the Northern soldiers refused to give up the fort to the Southern soldiers. The South attacked the fort and in two days took it. The great Civil War—the war between the Northern and the Southern states—had begun. President Lincoln called soldiers to the armies of the North; the South gathered its armies. They met in battle.

The war lasted for four long years. It was a very terrible war, and hundreds of thousands of young men on both sides lost their lives. There was sorrow and suffering and death. It was made worse because often families were divided, one member supporting the Northern side and another member the Southern side. Sometimes brothers fought against brothers. The North was unfortunate, in the beginning, in its choice of officers to lead the armies. The Southern soldiers were very brave. Battles were fought in the north, the south and the west, and sometimes one side was victorious and sometimes another. At one time the Southern army was within sight of the city of Washington. Then it was driven back. The war went on, year after year. Would it last for ever?

In the White House Abraham Lincoln quietly, sadly and ably guided the nation. Men complained about him, and he listened quietly and without anger. Men worked against him, and he did not turn against them. His great heart was full of grief; he loved peace; he was strong and determined to go on to the end. Slowly the ordinary people of the country began to know that in the White House there was a great President and a great man.

Lincoln had one serious fault, one which often troubled the officers of the army very much. He loved people, and he could understand and forgive their weaknesses, perhaps more than was best. He found it difficult, for example, to permit the army courts to have a soldier shot for running away during a battle or for falling asleep while on guard duty. He wanted to forgive them and give them a second chance, and their officers didn't like it. A mother's tears, a baby's cry, a story of misfortune—these touched his heart.

Lincoln and the Soldier

The following is an example of this so-called weakness of the President's. One day an army captain and a few soldiers came to see Lincoln at the White House. A young soldier had been found sleeping while on guard; he had been tried by the army court and ordered to be shot. Could the President please do something about it? A few hours later, the boy, now a prisoner in his tent, was surprised to receive a visit from the President of the United States, who, as President, was also head of all the Northern armies. Lincoln asked the boy about his home, his life on the farm and looked at the picture of his mother which the boy had with him.

"You are too good a boy to be shot for falling asleep only once. I grew up on a farm myself. But if you are set free you will have to pay heavily for it."

The boy's face brightened and he said: "I am sure that my father will be so happy, Sir, that he will gladly sell part of his farm and get the money."

"No," said the President, "that will not be enough. Only *you* can pay the bill, and pay only by proving yourself to be as brave and faithful as any soldier of the Union." His hand rested on the head of the boy, and his kind eyes looked full into the honest face. The boy promised.

The young soldier paid the bill very soon afterwards. In a fight with the enemy he jumped into a river to bring several wounded soldiers to the shore. Then he himself was shot, and died soon after. While dying he blessed the mercy of his President, for having given him this chance to die for his country.

Freeing the Slaves

Abraham Lincoln hated slavery, but he did not believe that the slaves should be freed suddenly and without the owners being paid. He knew that to do so would harm the South. For him this was first of all a war to keep the Union together. "If I could save the Union," he wrote, "without freeing any slaves, I would do it . . . and if I could save it by freeing all the slaves, I would do it. . . . What I do about slavery and the coloured race, I do because I believe it helps the Union." As the war went on, however, he came to believe that no nation could continue half slave and half free, and that slavery must cease. Something must be done about it. So, during the war he put his name to a paper, a very important paper, making free all the slaves in the states at war with the Union. This meant that from three to four million slaves were declared to be free, and that when the war was over they would be free.

The Gettysburg Speech

One of the great and bloody battles of the war was the battle of Gettysburg. Here the Southern armies were beaten and driven back into the South, but not until many thousands of brave men on both sides had lost their lives. They were buried where they fell. Later a great meeting was held on the battlefield of Gettysburg to honour the brave dead. Thousands of people came from miles around to the meeting, and to hear the two speakers, Mr. Everett and President Lincoln. Mr. Everett was a man of wide experience, the president of a college, one who had travelled much, a fine speaker. He spoke for two hours. Lincoln rose to speak. He had given but little thought and time to what he was to say, and had only just finished writing the end of his speech before riding out to the field. He stood before the great crowd, tall and thin, his sad face showing the sorrow of the war. He was silent for a moment, and then, as though he did not see the crowd, he spoke slowly, in a high voice, for three minutes. Before some of the people hardly knew he had begun, he had finished and sat down. One of the men sitting beside Mr. Everett turned to him and said: "He has made a failure and I am sorry for it. His speech was not equal to him." It was only when they saw it written, and read it for themselves that people began to know what it really was. Its simple and beautiful English, its noble meaning and forgiving spirit, make it one of the greatest speeches of the world. Its famous ending is well known: ". . . that this nation, under God, shall have a new birth of freedom—and that government of the people, by the people, for the people, shall not perish from the earth."

The End of the War

The years went by. In 1864 Lincoln was elected President for a second time. He had enemies who would have liked to see him beaten, but the common people believed in him and he began another four years in the White House. But now the war was coming to a close. The Northern armies were stronger; their leaders were more able now than earlier. The Southern armies were slowly driven back. As he saw the end of the war coming closer, the President began to make his plans. His task would soon be to see how the beaten states could be drawn back into the Union. His task would be to see how people who had hated and killed one another for four years could be made to understand one another and work together. It would be hard, but he, as President, must lead his people.

Death

But it was not to be. Forces were at work that would not allow him to carry out his dreams and plans. A young man, John Booth, who hated the North, had long planned to kill the President. The Northern victories made him hurry his plans. On the evening of April 14, 1865, Mr. and

The shooting of Lincoln

Mrs Lincoln went to the theatre in Washington. Booth was ready; he had made careful arrangements. Quietly he entered, held his pistol against the back of the President's head and fired. Then, striking with a knife a young man who tried to stop him, he jumped down among the actors, and escaped on a horse standing waiting at the theatre door. Mr Lincoln was carried to a house across the street and doctors hurried to his bedside. He died the next morning.

It is not possible to describe the feelings of the people as the terrible news of their President's death reached them. Strong men wept without shame. Even the people of the South were sorrowful, for they knew that they, too, had lost a friend. His body was carried by train to Springfield,

Illinois, following very much the same way as the train bringing him to Washington four years before. In every city and town and village the silent crowds gathered in sorrow and respect. This great man, beginning life in a log cabin and ending life in the White House, had won a place in the hearts of his people as no man before or since.

Four

MADAME CURIE

MARYA SKLODOVSKA was born in Warsaw, Poland, in 1867. Her father was a teacher in a school for boys, and for many years her mother was the head of a school for girls. Both were unusually fine people, and their children were fortunate in growing up in a home so filled with family love and with respect for books and study. They were Polish, and at a very early age the young Marya learned to love her country very much. This was at a time when it was dangerous to have feelings like this. Russia ruled a part of Poland, and the Czar of Russia was cruel to the Polish people. The Russians wanted their own language to take the place of the Polish language, and teachers were forbidden to teach the Polish language or Polish history in the schools. One of the events of Marya's early life, which she always remembered later, happened in a classroom at school.

Danger in the Classroom

A schoolroom of girls was busy studying history, but Polish history and in the forbidden Polish language. Suddenly a bell rang, two long rings and two short rings. This was a sign from the man at the gate of the school that someone was coming. Quickly the dangerous books were gathered up and carried away to a safe hiding-place; the girls picked up their sewing. The door opened and in walked a proud government officer. The sewing was laid aside. The officer wished to ask a few questions of one of

Marie Curie

the girls. And who could answer questions as well as Marya, who, although two years younger than the others in the classroom, knew the Russian language well, and was so clever? Marya was chosen.

"Repeat your prayer," said the officer in a loud voice. Marya gave it. "Now name the Czars of Holy Russia. . . . Who are the members of the Czar's family and what are their titles? . . . Who rules over us?"

The answers came clearly and correctly from the white-faced little Polish girl. The officer left the room, satisfied. "Come here, my little one," said the teacher to Marya. Marya left her place and came up to the teacher, who, without saying a word, kissed her. Marya burst into tears.

The Early Years

When Marya was ten years old her mother died, a great loss to the father and Marya and her two sisters and little brother. The older sister, Bronya, did her best to take the place of the mother and to give them a mother's love and comfort. But the loss of her mother whom she loved so much, and the earlier loss of a sister, grieved Marya. She found it difficult to understand how a God who was supposed to be good could so cruelly hurt her.

Marya learned her lessons quickly and easily. She was unusual in two ways. In the first place she had an excellent memory. By reading a poem only two times, she could say it aloud without a mistake. This so surprised her friends that they thought she had learned the poem secretly before. Because she was able to finish her studying quickly, she had time to help her friends with their lessons.

In the second place, she could shut herself off from all noise about her when she was reading a book. This is shown in the following happening. One evening Marya was seated at a big table in her home and all around her the young people of the house were shouting and making a terrible noise. But not once did the little girl raise her eyes from the book. She did not hear. Then, to have some fun with her, they built a bridge of chairs around her and over her. Still she made no sign. They waited, and for half an hour nothing happened. Then, when Marya finished the book, she closed it, raised her head ... and *crash!* All the chairs fell noisily to the floor, while all except Marya shouted with pleasure.

Her youth passed. Her father did not get much money; so in order to bring more money into the family Marya began to give lessons to children in their homes. It was not easy work for a girl of seventeen. There were long walks across the city in the rain and cold; there were careless and lazy children. There were mothers who made her wait in the hall, sending word by a servant: "Tell Miss Sklodovska to wait; my daughter will be there in fifteen minutes." There were mothers who were careless and forgot to pay her at the end of the month and kept her waiting for the much-needed money.

The "Floating University"

In order to satisfy her desire to learn after her excellent work at school had been completed, she studied in the "Floating University". This was a group of young people who met secretly to study university subjects. They met, a few at a time, in different homes and at different hours, and were taught by teachers who, like themselves, believed in planning for the future life of the Polish people. The Russian government had forbidden such meetings, and if the police had discovered them they would all have gone to prison. The aim of the "Floating University" was not only to teach the young people, but these young people were supposed to teach others.

Marya loved her sister Bronya, who had taken care of her like a mother, and she wanted very much to help Bronya to carry out her great aim in life. This was to go to Paris to study to be a doctor, and then to return to Poland, to work there. Marya, in her desire to help Bronya find a way, forgot that she too had at times had a dream of going to Paris to continue her studies.

Marya and Her Sister

One day Marya came to her sister with a plan. "Bronya, I've been thinking, and I've talked with father. I think I've found a way."

"A way?"

"Yes, a way. How many months could you live in Paris, with the money that you have saved?"

"I have enough money to pay for my journey to Paris, and the cost of living for one year. But it takes five years of study to become a doctor, as you know very well."

"Yes, Bronya, but we could work together, for each other. If we keep on struggling, each separately, neither of us can ever get away from Warsaw. But with my plan you can take a train this autumn."

"Marya, are you mad?"

"No. To start with, you will spend your own money. After that I will arrange to send you some, and father will, too. At the same time, I will be storing up money for my future studies. When you are a doctor it will be my turn to go and you will help me."

Bronya's eyes filled with tears at the goodness of the offer of her sister. And then she said, "But how can you possibly get enough money to help me and yet save some for yourself?"

"That's where my plan comes in," was the answer. "I'm going to get a position as a governess in a family. With food and lodging provided free I shall be able to save most of the money I get. So, everything is settled."

"But why should I go first, and not you?"

"Oh, Bronya, don't be silly! You are twenty years old and I am seventeen. You have been waiting for hundreds of years, and I have plenty of time. When you become a rich doctor, you can bury me in gold; in fact, I shall expect you to do just that."

The Governess

So Bronya went off to study in Paris, and in September, 1885, a silent young girl was looking for a position as a governess in a family. She went to a place where employment of all kinds was found for people. A woman clerk questioned her about the subjects which she had studied, the languages which she could speak, the sort of position she wanted. Then Marya went back home and waited.

A few months later we find her living in a large house in the flat country sixty miles from Warsaw, a governess to a little girl of ten. A new life of hard but pleasant work now began for her. During her long stay with the family she did not give up her books, but her work with the children of the home used up much of her strength. Two events of her life here are especially interesting.

One is that she began to teach some of the village children who lived near the house to read and write Polish. Two hours a day were given to this task, the teaching of from ten to eighteen poor children. They were not very clean and they were not very clever, but they were eager to learn. Great was Marya's joy, and that of the fathers and mothers of the children, when the letters and words of the book began to "talk" to those who had studied them so hard. Marya gave little attention to the fact that if the police had known of her little school she would have been sent to prison or far away, out of Poland.

The Young Man

The second event was of a different kind. The oldest son of the family came back from Warsaw for the holidays. He found in the house a charming governess, one who could dance beautifully and was good at playing games. He found a young lady who was clever and had good manners, one who could write poetry as easily as she rode a horse. He found a girl who was different from other girls he knew. They fell in love. They made their plans to marry, and the young man went to his father and mother to ask their permission. The answer was not long in coming. Father became very angry; Mother almost fainted. Their son, their dearest child, to marry this girl! She had no money at all; she was forced to work in other people's houses. To them a marriage with this girl was impossible! Marya's good family was not considered, nor her own character and charm. To the family of the young man the simple fact was just this: their son must not marry a girl who was a governess. The young man was weak; he changed his mind. Marya's feelings were hurt; she gave up love for always!

It was about this time that she wrote the following lines in a letter to her brother. He had left Warsaw and she wanted him to return there to continue his studies. She wrote: "Now that I have lost the hope of ever being worth anything in the future, all my life's purpose lies in Bronya and you. You two, at least, must make the most of your lives. The more sorry I feel because I cannot make more of my life, the more hope I have in you." She was at that time forcing herself to continue in her position as a governess in order that she might send half of what she was paid to her brother who was studying in distant Paris. Her feelings at this time are of special interest when we consider the fame which was one day to come to her.

Back to Warsaw

Three years had passed since Marya became a governess; these three years seemed long because they seemed without a purpose. But already small events were happening in Paris and Warsaw that were going to change her life. Her father, although no longer young, left his position in the boys' school and found a more difficult position that brought him more money. At once he began to save money for his oldest daughter, now reaching the end of her five years of study in Paris. Marya left her position as governess in the country and returned to Warsaw to live with her father. Again she became a student in the "Floating University", this time secretly doing experiments in the sciences. But now she began to feel, as her fine, clever hands did the experiments in this forbidden place, that here was her life work. She felt herself being forced on towards a purpose that was slowly forming in her mind.

Just at this time her sister in Paris wrote, urging her to join her there. Bronya had married, and her own university studies were almost at an end. She not only did not need any more help from her father and sister, but she invited the younger sister to live during the first year with her and her husband in their home. At first Marya was not certain what she ought to do. Then, a little later, she counted up the money which she had been able to save. Her father added a little more, and her mind was made up. She would go.

Off to Paris

In the autumn of 1891 we find Marya, now twenty-four years of age, saying good-bye to her father at the railway-station in Warsaw. "I shall not be away long . . . two years, three years. . . . As soon as I have finished my studies and a few examinations, I'll come back. Then we shall live together and never be separated again. Isn't that right?"

"Yes, my little Marya," he said with tears in his eyes and his arms about her. "Come back quickly. Work hard. Good luck!"

She took her place in the box-like car of the train, for she was paying as little money as possible for her journey. She sat silent in her uncomfortable seat as the train rushed across Germany, bearing her on to Paris, on to her sister, on to her life-work. She did not know that when she entered the train she had at last chosen between darkness and light, and was on her way to become a famous woman.

She reached Paris, and a few weeks later a simply and rather poorly dressed young Polish woman became a student in the famous French university. Marya Sklodovska the Polish governess was now Marie Sklodovska, a student of the sciences.

The Paris Home

She did not remain very long in the home of Bronya and her husband. It was too far from the university, and (even more important) in the home she could not give enough time to study. We have a picture of a young woman who was quiet, graceful and pretty, all of whose waking hours were used for study. She spent almost no money, just the amount necessary to pay for her room, her food, her clothes, her books and her university classes. She moved to a very small room at the top of a building, lighted from a small window in the roof. It was furnished with a small bed, one chair, a table, a bowl for washing, a stove on which to cook and an oil lamp for light. This was her home. She seems to have decided never to give up her Warsaw dresses, for she wore them for months and years.

Marie seemed to believe that she could not be cold or hungry. Sometimes, during the cold winter months, in order not to buy coal, which cost money, and sometimes because she did not want to take the time from her studies, she did not light the little stove. She continued her work without noticing that her fingers were getting stiff and that her shoulders were shaking. Hot *soup* would have comforted her, but she did not know how to make soup. Besides, soup would have cost money, and, above all, soup would take time to prepare. So for days and days she had nothing but bread and butter and tea. When she wanted a feast she would go into a shop and get two eggs or buy some sweets or some fruit. Eating only this food, she became very thin and weak. Often her head seemed to turn round and round, and sometimes she had just time to reach the bed and fall fainting upon it.

Hunger

Then one day she fainted in front of one of her friends, and her sister's husband, who was a doctor, was told about it. He hurried up the stairs to the little room under the roof, where a girl was studying her lessons for the next day. He looked at her and then looked about the almost empty room. The only food in the room was a packet of tea.

"What have you eaten today?" he demanded.

"I don't know. I ate some time ago."

"What did you eat?"

"A little fruit, and . . . a lot of things."

In the end she told him that since the evening before she had eaten nothing except a little fruit and some uncooked vegetables. She had worked until three o'clock in the morning, had slept for four hours and then had gone to her classes. When she returned from the university she had finished eating the vegetables; then she had fainted.

She was carried off to Bronya's home, dissatisfied and unhappy to leave her work. There she was made to eat the food which her weak body so much needed, and some of her strength returned. After several days she went back to her own room, promising to take better care of herself in the future. And the next day she began again to live . . . on air.

Yet to her these hurried and busy years were not the happiest but the most perfect in her life. She was young, she was alone and she enjoyed her studies. She found that one may be very happy in life even if one does not have money or even have enough food to eat. She was so interested in her work that she forgot about other things. Working in her little room at night, she felt herself in some mysterious way to be a companion of the great scientists of the past. Like her they were separated from the world about them, giving all their attention and all their strength to the search for knowledge.

Cold

Sometimes the Paris winter was longer than usual and the room under the roof was so cold that she could no longer sleep. She was cold, very cold, and her supply of coal was finished. But what of that? Could a Polish girl be conquered by a Paris winter? At such times she put on all the clothes she could wear, placed on the bed all her extra clothes, and then crept into bed. She was still cold. So, reaching out an arm, Marie pulled her chair on to the bed. This seemed to give a feeling of weight and heat. All she had to do now was to wait for sleep to come, without moving, of course, in order to preserve the mountain resting upon her. At the same time the layer of ice in the bottle of water on the table was growing thicker and thicker.

Her Marriage

All day and late at night she studied French, studied the sciences, worked in the laboratory. Sometimes, for a change, she took a bicycle ride out into the country, where she greatly enjoyed the flowers and the grass and the trees. She had need of nothing else, or at least so she thought. She certainly had no need of love, which she had left behind her some years before. She was surprised, therefore, to find that she was beginning to like very much a fellow scientist who was working in the laboratories, a certain Pierre Curie. He was a French scientist who had done much work in the kind of science which interested her. They came to know each other very well, to respect each other and then to love each other. In 1895 they were married. For a few days after their marriage they left Paris and went on a journey out into the country. They rode along the narrow lanes, Pierre in front, Marie coming along behind. As they rode along or walked together in the woods, they talked about science and their plans for improvements in their laboratory work. Then they went back to Paris and hard work.

The New Home

But marriage brought new duties to Marie. Their little home now had three rooms, high up at the top of a building and looking out over a garden. There was not much furniture in their main room, just enough for their needs, and they did not want any more. If anyone was so bold as to climb the many stairs to visit them, he found a small room with shelves of books, a table, some flowers and two chairs. And the chairs were not for him! They were occupied by the two Curies, who looked up from their studies in polite surprise.

Marie had meals to prepare. Before her marriage she did not take care of herself, but now she had a husband to care for. Now she must learn to make soup, and she did learn to make it and many other things besides. She got up early in the morning to buy vegetables in the market, and quickly learned to prepare simple food that would cook itself during the hours they were away during the day. But cooking must not take too much time, for there were more important things to do in the laboratory.

Eight hours of work in the laboratory were not enough. In the evening they sat down, one at each end of the table, with the lamp between, and became lost in their scientific studies. Until two or three o'clock in the morning the only sound was that of a moving pen or a turning page. Two years later their first child was born, a daughter, Irene, who was one day to win a Nobel Prize. Being a mother

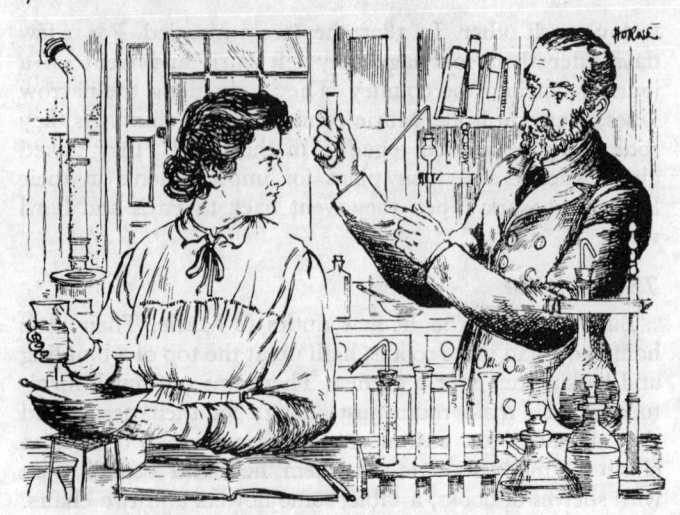

Marie and Pierre Curie in their laboratory

brought still more duties, but Marie carried on with her work, a good and happy mother and a wise and happy scientist.

In the Laboratory

At home, Marie the wife and mother, bathed her baby daughter and did the work of the house. In the laboratory, Marie the scientist was making one of the most important discoveries of science. A few years before, a certain scientist had discovered that a metal called uranium gave a kind of radiation, which Marie Curie was later to call radio-activity. But where did this radiation come from and what was it like? Here was a secret of nature which she set out to discover. Only a scientist could understand all that this pursuit meant. The experiments were done most carefully again and again. There was failure, success, more failure, a little success, a little more success. She repeated her experiments once, twice, ten times, twenty times. All seemed to prove that in the mineral which she was examining there was something, some form of radiation which man knew nothing about.

Four years before this, Marie had expressed her thoughts in words much like these: Life is not easy for any of us. We must work, and above all we must believe in ourselves. We must believe that each one of us is able to do something well, and that, when we discover what this something is, we must work until we succeed. This something in Madame Curie's own life was to lead science down a new path to a great discovery.

Working Together

At this time her husband left his own laboratory work, in which he had been very successful, and joined with her in her search for this unknown radiation. From this time on they were working so closely together that when they wrote articles on science to be printed they always wrote: "We did this," or "One of us did that." In 1898 they declared that they believed there was Something in nature which gave out radio-activity. To this Something, still unseen, they gave the name radium. All this was very interesting, but it was against the beliefs of some of the scientists of that day. These scientists were very polite to the two Curies, but they could not believe them. The common feeling among them was: "Show us some radium and we will believe you."

In order to show this radium and to prove that their ideas were right, Marie and Pierre Curie were to work for four long years.

There was an old building at the back of the school

where Pierre Curie had been working. Its walls and roof were made of wood and glass. It was furnished with some old tables, a blackboard and an old stove. It was not much better than a shed, and no one else seemed to want it. The Curies moved in and set up their laboratories and workshops. Here for four very difficult years they worked, every moment they could spare, weighing and boiling and measuring and calculating and thinking, and then thinking and calculating and measuring and boiling and weighing. They believed that radium was hidden somewhere in the mass of mineral dirt which was sent to them from long distances. But where? And could they find it?

The shed was hot in summer and cold in winter, and when it rained, water dropped from the ceiling. But in spite of all the discomfort the Curies worked on. For them these were the four happiest years of their lives. They worked week after week, and month after month, and year after year. They came nearer and nearer to the end.

Success

Then, one evening in 1902, as husband and wife sat together in their home, Marie Curie said: "Let's go down there for a moment." It was nine o'clock and they had been "down there" only two hours before. But they put on their coats and were soon walking along the street to the shed. Pierre turned the key in the lock and opened the door. "Don't light the lamps," said Marie, and they stood there in the darkness. "Look! . . . Look!" And there, glowing with faint blue light in the glass test-tubes on the tables, was the mysterious Something which they had worked so hard to find . . . Radium.

Unwelcome Fame

With the discovery of radium, fame came to the Curies, and they did not enjoy it. The two great scientists had discovered a secret of nature, and later they were to make other discoveries and give them to the world. And how did the world repay them? By giving them the things they wanted most? In fact, the only things they wanted . . . a good laboratory and peace and quiet? It did not. Every day they received letters inviting them to big dinners and important meetings. Every day they received letters inviting them to write articles for the newspapers, to lecture at public meetings, even to give money to unknown persons. Men from the Paris newspapers came into their little home to take photographs of everything, from the baby to the cat, and to ask their opinion on all sorts of subjects. For the Curies all this was a most painful experience, from which they did their best to escape, and never completely succeeded. It left its mark upon them. For many years, when strangers stopped her on the street to ask, "Aren't you Madame Curie?" Marie would answer in a cold voice, mixed with fear, "No, you are mistaken."

Jewels and Laboratories

One event shows us clearly in what the two scientists were really interested. A year after their discovery they were invited to England, where Monsieur Curie gave a speech on radium at a meeting of famous scientists. In the evening there was a large gathering which was attended by the scientists and their wives, and on the necks of the ladies there were diamonds and other costly jewels. Marie looked at the lovely jewels with pleasure and real admiration. She was rather surprised, though, to see that her husband, who usually did not notice such things, was also looking at them. Later that evening, when they were alone, Madame Curie said to her husband: "Pierre, I didn't imagine there were such jewels in the world! How pretty they were!"

Pierre laughed. "Do you know that during dinner, when I didn't know what to think about, I discovered a game. I figured out how many laboratories could be built with the money that those precious stones cost. By the end of the evening the number had become so high that I couldn't count any more."

The Nobel Prize

Later in the same year the two Curies received the Nobel Prize in physics. The Prize was sent to them, as they were unable at that time to go to Sweden to receive it. Both were far from well in health and both were too busy with their teaching and their laboratory. It was a great honour, one of many they were now receiving. But the honour meant very little to them. They found the Prize of value because the money they received made it possible for them to give up some of their teaching and to give more time to their scientific work.

But before this, something very important happened. Radium was found to be of help in destroying a terrible disease called cancer, and the knowledge of how to produce radium was worth a lot of money. One morning Pierre Curie came to his wife with a letter in his hand. "We must talk a little about our radium," he said. "Soon the whole world will be wanting radium. In this letter some people in America have written to ask our help in producing it, and will pay for it. We must decide what we are going to do. We can keep our knowledge to ourselves, as a secret which we own and can sell for a large amount of money. Or we can give our knowledge to the world as scientists do. We must decide carefully. Our life now is hard and may always be hard. We have a daughter to think of and we may have other children. The money we could get would bring us comfort, and . . . we could have a new laboratory, too."

A Great Decision

Marie's answer was not long in coming. She thought a moment and then said: "But scientists always give their discoveries to the world. It makes no difference that our discovery is worth money. We cannot sell it. It would be against the scientific spirit."

Silence followed. And then Pierre expressed the feelings of them both by repeating her words: "No, it would be against the scientific spirit."

Fifteen minutes later they were on their bicycles and riding in the direction of the forest outside the city. And in the evening they returned, tired out, their arms filled with bright-coloured leaves from the trees and flowers from the fields.

Fame and Children

Fame troubled Marie Curie and also her husband, because science was their world and in this world of science fame and honour to persons had no value. One day when a writer for a newspaper tried to ask Marie about herself and her thoughts and her beliefs, she answered him: "In science we must be interested in things, not in persons." Much of the real character and spirit of this unusual woman is found in these few words, which she was later often to repeat. One evening, at a big party, a friend asked her if she would not like to meet the King of Greece, who was also a guest. She answered in her simple manner: "I don't see the value of it." Then, seeing that she had hurt the feelings of her friend, she quickly added: "But . . . but . . . of course, I shall do whatever you please. Just as you please."

The months passed. Fame still troubled them; they both worked too hard, but life was a little easier. Their second daughter, Eve, was born, and the mother and scientist divided her time between the home and the laboratory and was happy in both. Monsieur Curie was invited to teach physics at the French university, but when he learnt that there would be no laboratory he refused. He would not accept the position until the government arranged to have a laboratory built.

Soon there were three helpers in this new laboratory, and Marie was their chief. Working in perfect union, Marie and Pierre Curie faced their future together.

Death of Pierre Curie

Then came April 19, 1906. Pierre Curie, walking along a crowded Paris street in the rain, slipped and fell. The wheels of a heavy truck passed over his body, and his life was gone.

The blow to Marie Curie was very great, so terrible that for a time her friends wondered if she would recover from it. Pierre's death left its mark upon her; she was never quite the same woman again. But life must go on . . . there were her two little girls, and there was her work, his work, their work. In the autumn of the same year there appeared a notice at the university, very short and simple, but it told much to those who knew the story behind it. The notice said that Marie Curie, wife of the famous scientist whose sad death had taken place a few months before, had been appointed to his position at the university and that she would give her first lecture the following Monday at half-past one in the afternoon. There was a crowd of people, besides the students, in the lecture hall that afternoon, all curious to see what she would do and hear what she would say. Would she praise her husband and his work? That would be a natural thing to do. Would she thank the government for the honour they were doing her in appointing her to her husband's place? That also would be a natural thing to do. Calmly and quietly she entered the room. And in a firm, unchanging voice she began her lecture just where her husband had ended: "When one considers the advance that has been made in physics in the past ten years. . . ." Tears came to the eyes of the people crowding the lecture hall, as she continued to the end and then left as rapidly and as silently as she had come in.

The First World War

Her life went on. In 1911 she received another Nobel Prize. In 1914 a new building was ready to be occupied, the Institute of Paris, a satisfactory and suitable place in which to continue her studies and experiments. But 1914 also brought war, the terrible First World War. France was in danger. One would expect a great scientist to feel that at such a time her place was in the laboratory. But when Paris was in danger Marie Curie quickly took her gramme of precious radium, no longer hers but belonging to the laboratory, and carried it to a safe place. Then she hurried back to Paris.

She knew that the newly discovered and invented X-ray machine would be of value to doctors who must treat the wounds of soldiers hurt in battle. With her help, such machines were placed in hundreds of hospital rooms in various parts of France. Others were placed in motor cars, and were moved from place to place as needed. These were laughingly called "little Curies", and Madame Curie herself was often seen driving one. The army doctors found the machines most useful, and by the end of the war hundreds of thousands of soldiers had received help through them.

What more can we say about this wonderful woman? She grew older and weaker. But all the time she was active in her work for science. In 1921 there was a journey to America. This journey followed the interesting visit of an American lady to Madame Curie in Paris.

The American Friend

A certain American lady, Mrs Meloney, had for many years admired Madame Curie from a distance and had always wished to meet her. Her wish was fulfilled when one morning she found herself in the presence of the great scientist in the laboratory in Paris, Mrs Meloney saw before her a woman dressed in a simple black cotton dress, with (as she later expressed it) "the saddest face I had ever looked upon". She tried to tell Madame Curie how interested the women of America were in her work and how proud they were of her. Soon they were talking about radium, and the scientist told her that there were fifty grammes of it in America. She went on to name the cities where the different amounts were to be found.

"And in France?" asked the visitor.

"My laboratory has hardly one gramme."

"*You* have only a gramme?"

"I? Oh, I have none. It belongs to my laboratory."

And then one more question from Mrs. Meloney, a silly one, perhaps, but one which was to be important: "If you had the whole world to choose from, Madame Curie, what would you take?"

And the answer from the scientist: "I need a gramme of radium to continue my laboratory work, but I cannot buy it. I have not enough money."

Mrs. Meloney returned to America with a plan taking shape in her mind. Madame Curie had discovered radium after years of labour and had given it to the world. Now she needed radium to be able to make more discoveries to give to the world. The world had radium and she had none, and she was too poor to buy some. So the world would buy it for her. In America Mrs. Meloney told the story of her meeting with "the woman in the black cotton dress". She told of her need, not for herself but for her laboratory. The people of America listened, and in less than a year the money was collected and the radium was bought.

Trip to America

Then followed the journey of Madame Curie and her two daughters to America to receive the gramme of radium, a present from the people of America. It was an interesting journey, but Madame Curie was now fifty-four years old.

She had not the strength to enjoy all the visits which she was expected to make to universities and laboratories and mines. She had not the strength to make all the speeches which she was expected to make nor to receive all the honours that grateful universities wished to give her. She was often too tired to attend a ceremony in her honour; and her daughters, Irene and Eve, had to take her place. More than once Eve, a girl of sixteen, listened with serious face as speeches prepared for her mother were addressed to her. They spoke of "your extraordinary work" and "your long life of labour", and the young girl had to make a suitable answer.

Gift from America

The most important ceremony took place in Washington, where the President gave her the radium in the name of the people of America. It was an interesting event and famous people were there. They, and the President as well, would have been very much surprised if they had known that Madame Curie had given away the radium before she received it. It happened like this. The evening before the ceremony Madame Curie learned from her friend Mrs. Meloney that the radium to be given the next day was to be a present to her, herself. She was troubled. The present must not be for her, but for science, for her laboratory. If it was owned by her, then after her death it would go to her daughters. It must be written down that it was for the laboratory. A lawyer must make the change, and at once.

"No, not next week," she said. "Not tomorrow . . . tonight. . . . I may die in a few hours."

So, with some difficulty a lawyer was found that evening. With his help the present of radium, not yet received by her, was given to the laboratory in Paris. The ceremonies and meetings were over at last. The visit to America came to an end. The three tired Curies returned to France.

The Last Years

In the years that followed, Madame Curie was active, but less so as the years went by and she grew weaker in body. There were visits to Poland, which she loved and which she continued to serve, and visits to her family and friends. There was more success and there were more honours. But most of the time she spent in the laboratory at the Institute of Paris, where she was loved by her fellow-workers, whom she helped by her example and her helpful advice.

She grew still weaker and could not leave her bed. Famous doctors were not certain at first what disease it was which was taking away her strength and her life. It was not like any other they had seen before. And then, towards the end, they knew. The strange disease was caused by radio-activity. Over the years the radium which she and her husband had discovered had harmed her body. During her last hours, and as she suffered, her mind wandered. She spoke about science, about her laboratory, about her studies, about radium. She died on July 4, 1934.

In a simple ceremony, and in the presence of only her close friends and the members of her family, she was buried in the grave beside her husband. To the stone that marked his grave a new line was added:

Marie Curie-Sklodovska, 1867—1934.

Her Gift to the World

As we look back over the years which have passed since the discovery of radium, we begin to see how much the world owes to Marie and Pierre Curie. For help in taking care of the sick under certain conditions, and in the understanding of growth in plants and animals, science cannot fail to thank Madame Curie. For making easier a study of the space beyond the sun and the stars, and for making simpler a study of the age of living things which lived countless years ago, science must honour Madame Curie. Even our knowledge of atomic energy (whether man chooses in the future to use it for good or for evil) has its beginnings in the results of the experiments in the simple shed in Paris where the two Curies laboured for four long years.

One of Marie Curie's best science students wrote at the time of her death: "We have lost everything." This was his feeling at the time of her death, but the feelings of the world in thinking of the life of this great woman and great scientist must be: "We have not lost everything. We have gained so very, very much."

Five

ALBERT SCHWEITZER

In the centre of Africa not long age there lived a doctor. He was over eighty years of age, and he had been working among the African people there for a very long time. But he was not born there; this was his second home. The life of this man was an interesting one and very unusual. It is of interest to old and young, to people of all religions and to people of all countries. Great men belong to the whole world, and Albert Schweitzer was one of the great men of the world. To understand his greatness one must follow his life from the time he was a little boy.

The Fight

It was a warm afternoon at the end of autumn and the little village of Gunsbach in Alsace lay as if asleep. But suddenly it became awake. The bell at the top of the church began striking four; the bell in the school began to ring. At the sound, the covers of classroom desks were shut as the school books were put away. There was a sound of wooden shoes moving swiftly across the classroom floor. School was over for the day and the children were going home.

Two little boys started out of the door. Then the taller of the two said: "You wouldn't dare to fight me, Albert Schweitzer. I'm too strong, and I could put you on your back any day, if I wanted to."

"That's what you say, George," said the smaller boy. "But I'd like to see you try it."

"Of course I could," said George.

"Come on then," said the smaller boy.

The two boys left the path and went into a field where the ground was soft and level. The battle began. George attacked first . . . a quick jump and he had caught Albert around the waist. They struggled hard to throw each other to the ground, breathing hard and using all their strength. Albert felt himself beginning to fall, but he pushed back hard. Then he suddenly let go of George's arm and seized his legs and pulled hard. George sailed through the air and fell. The next thing he knew he was lying on his back in the grass. And Albert was sitting on his stomach, laughing happily down at him.

"How did you like that, George?" he said laughingly and breathing with difficulty. "I put you down, didn't I?"

George searched for words to comfort his pride. "All right, young Schweitzer, you win," he said. "It's easy for you. You're the minister's son and a little gentleman. Have you ever been hungry? If I had good soup for supper two times a week, like you, I'd be as strong as you are."

Silence. Then, without a word Albert Schweitzer got up from George's chest and picked up his school books. Without a word he started off down the road.

"Albert, Albert, come back," called George. "Don't be angry." Everybody liked the minister's son, and already George was sorry for what he had said. But Albert did not even turn his head and was soon out of sight.

When Albert Schweitzer reached home he went straight to his bedroom, and the rest of the family did not see him until supper-time. Then the father, the mother and the five children . . . two boys and three girls . . . gathered around the supper table. The father spoke a short prayer: "Praise God for He is good; His mercy is without end."

"What's for supper, Mother?" called out one child.

"It's soup," said another. "I thought it would be soup. Good!"

"Here, Albert," said his mother, "here's a big bowl of

Albert Schweitzer

soup for you. You're the oldest and you're always hungry after school."

Albert said nothing but sat looking at the dish in front of him. He was hearing, not the friendly words of his family, but the clear voice of his friend George: "If I had good soup for supper two times a week, like you, I'd be as strong as you are." He looked at the soup in his plate, raised a spoonful to his mouth and tried to swallow it. He could not. "I'm not hungry," he said.

"Not hungry?" said his mother. "Do you feel ill?"

"No, I'm all right, Mother, just not hungry. Please may I go to my room?"

He left and they finished supper without him. Alone in his room he made a promise to himself: "I won't be different from the other boys any more, or do anything to make them feel I have more than they do. I want us to be real friends."

Home Life

The Schweitzer family was a happy one most of the time. Brothers and sisters played happily together, and their friends were always welcome in their home. Mrs Schweitzer worked hard, cooking the food for the large family and caring for the house. But she was always glad to have the children playing in and out of the house.

Mr Schweitzer was the pastor of the village church, and much loved and respected by the people. As a pastor he received very little money, and it was necessary for them to live simply. But he felt that it was important for his children to dress well. This feeling led to a serious misunderstanding between him and his son Albert.

One Sunday morning, as the family was getting ready for church, Mrs Schweitzer came into the room with a boy's winter coat on her arm. "Look, Albert," she said. "See what I have for you. Your father has at last bought a new winter coat and this old coat has been made smaller so that it will fit you. It looks almost new."

Albert's face grew red. "I don't need it today, Mother. It really isn't cold enough."

"But, child, it is very cold," said his mother. New clothes were not common in the Schweitzer family, and she was surprised to find that Albert was not pleased.

"Mother, please don't make me wear it. None of the other boys in the village have winter coats. I don't want to be different from them."

He did not wear the coat that day. When his mother saw him start for school the next morning, she was surprised and not pleased. Albert was not wearing the coat, but he was wearing wooden shoes, and on his head was a village boy's cap. She spoke to her husband about it, and Albert was called to the room where his father was at work writing.

"Now, my boy," said Mr. Schweitzer, laying down his pen, "your mother works hard to see that you have clothes to wear and food to eat. You should show how grateful you are by wearing clothes which are suitable for the son of a minister."

"But I don't want to be——" began Albert. Then he stopped when he saw his father pick up his pen and turn to his writing.

"I hope, if only for your mother's sake, that you will do as I say and wear the clothes we provide for you. That is all." Albert went out.

This was the beginning of a struggle between father and son which lasted for a long time. The father felt that he should be obeyed and that his son should wear the winter coat. The son felt just as strongly that he could not and would not be different from the poor boys with whom he played and who had no winter coats.

The boys of the village never knew what a struggle Albert had at home, nor how often he was punished—and all because he felt that if they couldn't have coats like his, then he didn't want one. The struggle went on for a long time. It ended only when the coat became too small for the growing boy to wear and it was laid aside for his younger brother.

School Life

The boys at school all liked Albert, but when they found that it made him angry to be called "the little gentleman", they found pleasure in using this name for him. In school he was not very clever; often his mind seemed to be anywhere else than in the classroom. He often came home and told his family that this boy or that boy was much better in lessons than he. Yet in almost every other way he was a son to be proud of, tall and strong and friendly.

But there was something in which he was far better than the other boys, and that was music. When he was a little boy of five his father gave him lessons on the piano which they had at home. Reading music and playing music seemed to him as natural as talking. What he liked most was to play on the piano, music that he had heard, or to make up his own simple music. At the age of eight he was allowed to take lessons on the organ. When he was only nine he played well enough to take the place of the man who played the organ in his father's church.

When he was nine he left the village school and went to a higher school in a village near their home. He had to walk a number of miles each day, but he did not mind this. He enjoyed being out of doors, and he enjoyed being alone, although he also liked people. The boys in his class found that it was easy to make him laugh and to laugh loud and long. They did funny things to make him laugh during the lesson. When this happened the master would take his pen and put a black mark in his book: "Schweitzer—for laughing in class." They called him "Laughter".

Love of Animals

Albert loved animals, and even when he was very young any cruelty was terrible to him. Once he saw a sick horse being driven along the streets of the village. The sight remained with him for weeks. When he closed his eyes in bed at night he saw the horse in the darkness and heard the blows of the stick driving it along. He could not understand why his father, in his prayers, prayed only for people. After Albert had gone to bed, he added a little prayer of his own: "Bless all things that have breath. Guard them from all evil and let them sleep in peace."

There came a time when he had to decide what to do when he saw this thing which he so hated . . . cruelty to animals. It happened as follows:

"Schweitzer! Look at what I've got." His friend Henry was calling to him, and showing him a simple weapon made from a forked stick with a piece of rubber tied between the two ends.

"That's a good one," said Albert, "I wish I had one like it." He took it in his hand and examined it carefully.

"I made this one. You can make one like it, too," said Henry.

They searched among the branches of the trees until they had found just what they wanted. A few minutes' work with a knife; a piece of rubber tied on; the weapon was ready for use.

"Now come," said Henry. "Let's go up on the hill and shoot birds." They found the birds, lovely little yellow ones with caps of red on their heads. Henry picked up a round stone and fitted it into the rubber. Albert did the same.

"Now watch me," said Henry as he took careful aim at a bird.

Suddenly the sound of church bells floated up from the valley below. The sweet sound of the bells joined with the sweet song of the birds. They brought back to Albert's mind the words that Sunday after Sunday he had heard his father read in church: "Thou shalt not kill." He knew at once what he must do. Raising his voice in a shout, he struck his hands together to drive the birds away. They rose in a cloud and were gone. Albert turned and ran home, without a word to his friend. From that time on he did not mind what others thought about it. He would not kill. He would not join his friends in hunting or fishing or in any game in which living creatures of any kind were killed.

The days and years passed. Schweitzer was not a very good student in school, but when he saw that his low marks were causing his parents real sorrow, he promised to do better. And he did do better, forcing himself to do tasks even when he got no pleasure from them. History was the subject which he liked best.

Music

His music lessons continued. With one of his teachers he did not practise enough and he played the piece of music without feeling. Part of this was because he was a boy and did not like to show his real feelings. One day, as he was playing in this manner, his teacher could bear it no longer.

"My beautiful Mozart!" he burst out. "You don't deserve to be given such a lovely piece of music to play!" He began to look for some music to give Albert for his next lesson. "What can I give you? Here, try this piece for next week. But if you haven't any feeling for music, I can't put it there."

Albert took the music to his home. "No feeling for music!" he said to himself. "So that's what he thinks of me!" For so long as he could remember music had been his greatest pleasure. That week he really practised. He studied the music with great care and practised it hour after hour. The next week he returned for his lesson.

"You are going to spoil this one for me, I suppose," said the teacher. Albert started to play. He played the piece simply and with feeling. When he finished, his teacher said, "Thank you." Nothing more. But from that time on things were different. The teacher opened up to the boy the world of music and taught him to enjoy it. He loved the music of Bach (a great German writer of organ music) best of all.

School Examinations

When young Schweitzer was eighteen years old his secondary-school work came to an end. The examinations at the end provided amusement for Albert's many friends, if not for himself. At this time he was living with his uncle and aunt in a village next to Gunsbach, in order to be able to attend the secondary school. As the time of the examinations came near his aunt said to him:

"Don't forget that for the examinations you must wear a black coat and black trousers with stripes. That is the custom."

"I have a black coat, but I haven't the trousers."

"Then you must have a pair made," said his aunt firmly.

"Oh no. Father doesn't have the money to spare for such clothes. The girls need new dresses. Couldn't I borrow a pair of yours, uncle?"

"What's that, my boy?" said his uncle, looking up from his newspaper. "Borrow my trousers? Of course, if they'll fit you. You had better try them on to see."

Albert had little interest in clothes and he forgot to try on the trousers. On the morning of the examination he took them out of the box and put them on. But Albert was tall and thin and his uncle was short and fat. You can imagine the effect. The bottom of the trousers reached half-way up his legs, and around the waist there was room for two Alberts. He did the best he could and went off to the examination. He found his friends gathered outside the examination-room. They were anxious about the examinations, but the sight of their friend changed everything. They burst into laughter and shouted that he looked like an elephant, and many other things. Even after they had entered the room and were facing the solemn examiners, someone would look at Albert and a low wave of laughter would go from one end of the room to the other. He was successful in his examinations though, and greatly pleased his examiners by his answers in history. Now he was ready for the university.

His studies at the University of Strasbourg began, and because of his great interest in them he found himself studying two main subjects. He was fortunate in being able to continue with his studying even when he was having his year of army training. While his soldier companions were spending their free time in pleasure and talk, the serious Schweitzer would be sitting apart busy with his studies.

Music Again

In the autumn of 1893 he visited Paris for the first time, and stayed at the home of his uncle. His main purpose was to see some of the famous old organs in Paris and to meet the famous French organ-player, Monsieur Widor. His aunt had arranged for him to play the organ for the great musician. She wanted to get his opinion on how well Schweitzer played and whether he should be advised to continue.

"What are you going to play for me?" asked Monsieur Widor as the young man burst into the room.

"Bach, of course," was the answer. Albert sat down before the organ, much larger and finer than any he had played on before. He began to play. As he heard the lovely sounds from the organ he forgot everything except the beauty of the music. The inner voices of each sound spoke to him. As for the master, he forgot, too—forgot that it was only out of kindness that he had been willing to hear this unknown country fellow play. He recognized in Schweitzer the beginnings of a great organ player.

"How soon can you come to me for lessons?" he asked when Albert finished. That was the beginning of a friendship between the two which was to last for ever. Whenever, in the years that followed, Albert was able to get to Paris, he took lessons from Monsieur Widor. When he had money he paid for his lessons; when he did not have money, then the lessons were gladly given free.

The Great Decision

When Albert Schweitzer was twenty years old, he made a very important decision. During the summer holidays he returned to the little village of Gunsbach. He was looking forward to the summer as a time to think about his future. What should he do with his life? Should he be a university professor, with lectures to give and books to write? Should he become a minister like his father, and settle down to a quiet and useful life in a village? Or should he become a great musician, as Widor was advising him to do? Often it is not easy for a young man to make such an important choice.

Then one morning he awoke early. It was a lovely day and the country had never seemed more beautiful. "All this is lovely," he thought. "But have I the right to it? What right have I got to be so happy when there is so much unhappiness in the world?" Even now, as when he was a small child, he was troubled by the sufferings of animals. He could not even bear to see animals in cages, walking up and down, up and down. But now that he had grown up he saw and understood the sufferings of people. The thought of it cast a shadow over the bright summer morning.

In thinking about it, he said to himself: "Here I am, twenty-one years old. I am as strong as a horse, with a happy home life behind me, and I have work that gives me pleasure. I love the country, my friends, my books, my music. What right have I to so much happiness?"

There came before his eyes the scene of years before, of his fight with George after school. He heard again the voice of George saying: "If only I had good soup two times a week like you. . . ." And then the voice of Henry saying: "Let's go up on the hill and shoot birds . . . !" This was followed by the clear sound of the church bells from the valley and the feelings that had come over him of pity for all helpless creatures.

"I have always been one of the lucky ones," he thought. "But what about the others? I tried to forget them; I wanted to live my life for myself alone. But it was no good. I can't enjoy my happiness while all the world round me is full of suffering."

And there, that morning in summer, his plans began to take form. He decided that until he was thirty years old he would spend his time studying and practising his music. After that he would give up his whole life to serving others. He dressed and went down into the garden for a walk before breakfast. He felt a new calm and peace; he now felt an inner, as well as an outer, happiness.

Schweitzer had decided to enjoy music and university work as fully as possible, until he was thirty. He was to fill the next nine years with enough action for several lifetimes.

He completed his studies at the university. He started work on several books two of which were about the great musician Bach. He gave talks at Strasbourg University. He was the head of a college, the minister of a church and he played the organ regularly. The study room in his house was filled with books and papers, much to the sorrow of the woman who cleaned the room. But she found him an easy man to work for, because he ate what was put before him and he never seemed to notice whether his clothes were mended or not.

All this time Schweitzer was looking for some kind of work in which he could spend his life. He early joined a group of young people who visited poor families regularly and helped them. In the group there was a young woman whom he came to know well and whom he was later to marry. The years went by. One evening, when he was twenty-nine, he went to his study room as usual. He picked up a paper which someone had placed on his desk and began to read. His eye fell on an article describing the needs of the Congo. He read about the tribes of black people in the centre of Africa, unhappy because of disease and lack of food. And there was no doctor, the article said, for hundreds of miles around. As he continued to read, he knew that here were people who needed help. His decision was made; his search was over. He would go to Africa to serve the black people, and since a doctor was what they needed, he would go as a doctor.

When he told his friends what he had decided to do, they could not believe him at first. Here was a man who could live a happy and useful life in Europe as a doctor, or as a university professor, or as a musician, or as a writer—and what was he planning to do? At the age of thirty he was planning to study medicine, and to bury himself in the centre of Africa, in one of the most unhealthy spots in the world. One could not believe it! He was mad! "But why, Albert," asked his friend Monsieur Widor, "if you must go to Africa, why not go as a minister? At least you are all ready for that!"

"I know," was Schweitzer's answer; "but a doctor is what they need out there. Besides," he paused, "I want to be able to help without talking. It's no use talking to people about a religion of love; they must see you practise it."

Studying Medicine

For the next five years he was again a student, studying medicine. The studying was difficult, but he worked hard, he enjoyed it, and he was successful in it. He spent another year getting experience in a hospital and raising money for the hospital he planned to have in Africa. He got the money from interested friends and by giving organ concerts in different parts of Europe. Then he married the young lady whom he had loved for a long time and who, while he had been studying medicine, had been training as a nurse. The last weeks before they sailed were spent in buying all sorts of supplies that they knew would be needed in their new work. In the spring of 1913, when Schweitzer was thirty-eight years old, the doctor and his wife went on board the ship that was to take them down the west coast of Africa.

Arrival in Africa

At the mouth of the Ogowe River they changed to a river-boat, and for two days and a night were moving slowly up the river, between the thick forests on either side. It was hot in the daytime; it was hot at night—terribly hot. They reached the village of Lambaréné, and changed to small log boats for the last short distance. The young black men stood in the dug-out tree trunks, so easy to turn over, and struck the water with their long narrow pieces of wood. Again and again they sang as they rowed: "Tzeh, poba-hoba, tzeh, tzut-tzut; tzeh, poba-hoba, tzeh, tzut-tzut."

The log boats moved into a little bay. The Schweitzers climbed the little hill to the rough houses above the river. This was to be their home for years to come. News had spread through the forest that a doctor had come to Lambaréné, and even before their boxes of medicines arrived on the river-boat, the sick people began to crowd around the house. Every morning when he stepped out of his house he found them waiting for him, thirty or forty coloured people sitting on the ground in the shade of the house. These were not the town Africans from the coast, but simple wandering people from the forest. Old people, young people, babies; men, women and children; ill with all kinds of diseases, weak from lack of food. "Here among us everybody is ill," said a young man; and an old chief shook his grey head sadly. "Yes, our land eats its own children." All their faces were turned towards Schweitzer for comfort; he was the only man for hundreds of miles who could help them.

When his boxes of supplies came there was no place to put them. For a time he cared for the sick people in the open air, and then ran for shelter when the heavy rains came pouring down. Things became better when he cleaned out an old hen-house and used this as the centre of his work. It was difficult not to begin to despair. There was so much to do. What could one man do against a whole world of suffering? During these first months his wife gave him help and strength. She worked as hard as he did—first caring for the house and giving orders to the untrained servants; then hurrying over to the hen-house to help the doctor with his operations and care for the sick.

Joseph

It was a happy day when the doctor found among the sick people a keen-looking coloured man who spoke French and who had been a cook to a white man. "Would you like to come to me as cook and also to help me in the hospital?" Schweitzer asked. The man's face brightened with pleasure. "Yes, Doctor," he said, "I will help you with everything."

That was the beginning of Joseph, who stayed with them for many years. He was an unusual man, kindly, keen, hard-working, honest. He could speak eight languages, and although he could not read or write French he never made a mistake in taking down a bottle of medicine from the shelf. "How do you know which one to take?" Schweitzer once asked him. "The bottles are nearly all the same."

"I remember the look of the words on the paper," was the simple answer. Joseph had said he would help with everything, and he did. It was Joseph who helped in the hospital, who translated for the Schweitzers, who helped them to understand the ways of Africa. If Schweitzer was angry when someone stole something from the house, it was Joseph who explained, with a bright smile: "You forgot to lock it up, Doctor; so of course it went for a walk."

Life at Lambaréné

Friends in Paris had given Dr. Schweitzer a very lovely present—a fine piano. This had come out by ship and had been carried ashore in one of the boats made from the trunk of a tree. For the first few months after his arrival it stood untouched in the living room. "No, don't ask me to play," he would say to his wife in the evenings. "Coming to Africa has meant the end of my life as a musician." But one evening he began to play, and from then on almost every evening the voice of music spoke in the forest. He had the time now to go on to a fuller knowledge and understanding of music, and especially of the noble music of Bach.

Before autumn came, two new rooms in which to examine the sick and to operate had been built. Also there were a number of rooms in which the sick could stay until they were well. All this was new to the sick, and also to their friends and members of the family who came with them. The first night, as the doctor went through the rooms for a last visit to the sick, he found a number of them lying on the floor while their healthy friends were enjoying the comfort of the beds. "What a difference," he thought as he made them move out and give the beds to the sick, "between this and the hospital at Strasbourg!"

Hospital Work

After some time, things were going well and the work went on. But what sorrow and suffering among the crowds that came from miles around! The sick had no knowledge of medicine except as a kind of magic. Schweitzer soon found that up and down the river the people thought of him as a powerful magician. The name Oganda, by which he was known, meant that he was able to do magic. "Indeed, he is great," said an old woman with trouble with her heart. "He knows I can hardly breathe at night and that I often have swollen feet, yet I didn't tell him and he never looked at my feet." They were much surprised by the way he put them to sleep when he operated on them. "Since Oganda has been here we have seen wonderful things," said a little girl. "First he kills the sick people, then he heals them, and then he wakes them up again."

After nine months Schweitzer was able to write to his friends in Europe that he had cared for more than two thousand people. The need was great. One day a man was brought in a log boat by his friends and carried up the hill to the hospital. His pain was terrible, yet he was only one of many who had to suffer until they died, unless the only doctor for hundreds of miles around could save them. Schweitzer went over to speak to the suffering man. "Don't be afraid," he said, laying his hand gently on the black head. "In less than an hour's time you will go to sleep, and when you wake up you won't feel any pain." The man was made ready, and the doctor, helped by his wife and the faithful Joseph, performed the operation. Later, Schweitzer sat by his bed waiting for him to wake. Slowly he moved a little, breathed deeply, rolled his head on the bed and came back to life. Suddenly his eyes opened. "I've no more pain," he said. He looked about him, fixed his eyes on the doctor, and repeated as if he could not believe it, "No more pain! No more pain!" His hand searched for Schweitzer's hand, held it and would not let go. "I've no more pain!" He was one of the many who, in the years that followed, were to feel the healing power of Oganda's hands and loving heart.

War

By the summer of 1914 the Schweitzers had spent two dry seasons in Africa, and Mrs Schweitzer was slowly becoming tired out from the climate and the difficult work. They planned to return to Europe for a change, as all white people working in this country must do. Then, in midsummer, a party of French soldiers came to the Schweitzer home. War had broken out in Europe. "You are Alsatians, born on German soil," they said. "This country is French. Our countries are at war. You may stay in your own home, but you are prisoners." The two Schweitzers obeyed quietly, but the sick in the hospital were angry. "You are not our doctor's masters," they said, and would have thrown stones at the soldiers if Schweitzer had not stopped them.

The doctor himself was troubled to think that war in Europe must stop his hospital work in Africa, and the simple African people could not understand at all what was happening.

"How many men have been killed?" asked one old black man, from a tribe that was known to have the custom of eating its enemies. "Ten?"

"Oh, many more than ten," was the answer.

"In our battles we have to pay for dead men. How will they ever pay for so many? Why don't their tribes meet and have a talk?"

The same old man asked: "Do the white men eat each other?"

"No, indeed, they do not."

"Then they must kill each other just because they are cruel."

Now that there was little that he could do at the hospital, Schweitzer began to do something which he had long wanted to do. He began his book about the meaning of life, and why we are in this world and what we must do.

He continued to write and write, pouring out his soul on paper. "Our world is sinking like an old boat," he said to himself. "I must help to build a new and better one, in which we can all travel through life." All around him he felt the struggle in nature, each plant and animal in the forest fighting for its life, just as he must fight for his. "Can we live only by destroying each other?" he thought. Out of his thinking came a firm belief that all life is holy and our duty is to care for it. "We must respect life. If a man has respect for life he will never thoughtlessly destroy any life, whether the life of man, or animals, or insects, or flowers, or leaves of a tree."

Back in Europe

Suddenly, in early autumn 1917, a change came. The two Schweitzers were ordered to return to France to enter a prison-camp. They packed very hurriedly, and said sad good-byes to their many black friends; then they went on to the boat which was to carry them to the coast. In the prison-camp in France they found themselves among prisoners from many nations. Here, as he was the only doctor, Schweitzer was able to make himself useful by taking care of the sick. He had many talks with other people in the camp, and learned about their former lives and occupations. He gained many new ideas, which he stored away in his mind for future use. The following spring a number of French prisoners held in Germany and an equal number of German prisoners held in France were allowed to return to their homes. The two Schweitzers were set free, and in a very short time were back once more in the little village of Gunsbach. His mother had been killed, but his father was still quietly at work in the village. The village itself was unhurt by war, although near the centre of fighting, for the hills had protected it. At the end of the war Alsace once again became a part of France.

After Schweitzer had recovered from two serious operations, which left him weak for some time, he found himself with an urgent question to answer. What should he do next? He owed money to pay for his operations, and he had borrowed money to buy supplies for the hospital in Lambaréné. Europe claimed him—he was known as a writer, as a doctor, as a musician, as a professor. He had so much to give. Friends and relations begged him to take up work in Europe. An excellent offer to teach in a university in Switzerland came to him. His wife's health had not recovered from their hard life in Africa. And now there was a baby daughter to be thought of. But—Lambaréné was calling, too. The letters came from the heart of the forest: "Doctor, they miss you." "Doctor, you must come back." "Please, Doctor." In his own mind the voices became the voices of the sick he had helped, the simple black friends who loved him and who needed him.

The question of money was taken care of. He travelled from country to country in Europe, playing the organ, and speaking to crowds of people about the work in Lambaréné. People listened to his music. They listened also as he told of the hospital in Africa. What he said was interesting enough, but those who heard him saw something more than an ordinary man: they saw a man who was filled with a spirit of service and love, and respect for life.

Africa Again

Once more, eleven years after his first coming, Schweitzer found himself in a boat moving slowly up the Ogowe River. His wife had been unable to go with him this time, but his companion was a young student of medicine who was going to help him. They reached Lambaréné, and Schweitzer hurried up the hill to see what time and the forest had done to the hospital. He looked—where were they? Most of the buildings had disappeared, broken down and swallowed up by the terrible strength of the African forest. Tall grass and trees covered everything.

Almost at once Schweitzer was at work, searching for workers to clear out the trees and grass and rebuild the huts. Long before the buildings were ready, the sick began to arrive. "He is back; he is here! The big doctor is here!" The happy news spread quickly, and soon the same circle of anxious black faces watched for him to appear at the door of his house each morning. It was a difficult time. Schweitzer struggled to see the sick in the morning, and to rebuild the hospital buildings in the afternoon. It was not easy to find workmen, and if he left them for five minutes they stopped working. He would find them lying in the shade, laughing and talking.

"It is your fault, Doctor," explained one of them; "you did not stay to watch us, so of course we did not work."

The years passed. Schweitzer made the journey between Lambaréné and France many times. He divided his life into times of work in Africa and even more difficult times of "rest" in Europe. In Europe he saw his friends, wrote his books and visited various countries. He gave talks about Lambaréné, and played the organ, all to gain friends and money for the hospital. In Lambaréné the number of workers increased and also the number of huts for the sick. The discovery of a spring of pure water was most important. The thick forest was cut back, and a garden was planted to give fresh fruit and vegetables for both workers and the sick.

In 1947 the hospital had three hundred and fifty beds for the sick, and it also had a group of trained and loyal doctors and nurses from Europe. It served all who needed their help, but the doctor himself became especially interested in helping those suffering from a serious disease called leprosy. There was new hope for those with this disease, for new medicines had been discovered. A special village was built near the hospital, where those who had this disease could be kept away from others and yet be near enough for the long care they needed.

The hospital at Lambaréné

Later Years

Today Lambaréné is an active centre of work, serving the needs of many thousands of people of that very hot and very wet part of Africa. The man who made it was as simple as ever, and as determined. Honours have come to him—the Nobel Prize, honours from universities and governments. His books on music and religion and the meaning of life have been praised in all parts of the world. He is recognized as one of the greatest organ players of all time. His noble spirit, his simple living, his unceasing work for others have given hope and strength to many people. He was a man who seemed to have everything, who gave it all away, freely, of his own choice, and then saw it in time given back to him. In a world which seems to have lost its way, he knew where he was going. Others have written and taught, but Schweitzer lived his teaching, at the cost of very great labour, for more than forty-four years.

He divided his life between Africa and Europe, but in him the two became one. In the thick darkness of the African night he played the same lovely music of Bach that he began to know while a young man in Alsace.

Albert Schweitzer died at Lambaréné in 1965.

The news of his death flashed around the world. He was one of the great men of our day.

QUESTIONS ON THE STORIES

ONE—MAHATMA GANDHI

His Home
1. What was Mahatma Gandhi's real name?
2. Where and when was he born?

At School
1. Why did Mohandas run home from school each day?
2. What kind of exercise did he take?

Marriage
1. At what age was Mohandas married?
2. Why were the three boys married at the same time?

Mistakes of Youth
1. Why didn't Gandhi want to eat meat?
2. Why did he at last stop eating meat?

In England
1. In London what difficulty did he at first have with food?
2. What did he do about it?
3. What holy books did he become interested in?

India Again
1. When did Gandhi return to India?
2. What sad news did he learn when he landed?

In South Africa
1. What happened one day when he was riding on a train?
2. Why did Gandhi begin to work to help the Indians in South Africa?

His Life-work Begins
1. What was "soul force"?
2. What success did Gandhi have during his years in South Africa?

India and Work for the Poor
1. What did people promise when they joined his ashram?
2. Why did the rich Hindu stop helping to support the home?

Self-government for India
1. What did he mean by saying, "We must earn it ourselves"?
2. When did he sometimes go for many days without food?

The End Draws Near
1. What terrible things happened?
2. Why did peace come sooner in the part of the country where Gandhi lived?
3. When and where was Gandhi killed?

TWO—FLORENCE NIGHTINGALE

Early Life
1. When and where was Florence Nightingale born?
2. Why was she named Florence?

Voices
1. What strange experience did she have when about sixteen years old?
2. How many times did this happen in her life?

First Plans
1. Whom was she allowed to nurse during these years?
2. From this work what important thing did she learn?

Beginning of the Crimean War
1. Where did the Russian and British armies fight?
2. Why did so many thousands of British soldiers die?

The Call Comes
1. Who wrote to Florence Nightingale about the Scutari hospital?
2. What did he want her to do?

Turkey
1. How did the party of nurses get to Constantinople?
2. Why was the sea voyage unpleasant for Miss Nightingale?

Hospital Conditions
1. From what did the wounded soldiers die?
2. What did the rules say about giving them new supplies?

Unwelcome
1. How did the doctors decide to treat the nurses?
2. What did Miss Nightingale decide to do about this?

Work Begins
1. What brought serious trouble to the British army?
2. Why did the doctors turn to Florence Nightingale?
3. How did she get the solders' clothes washed?

Florence in Charge
1. How did she get the hospital repaired?
2. Why did some of the nurses dislike Florence?

Visit to the Crimea
1. What happened to her in the Crimea?
2. How did the soldiers receive this bad news?

Difficult Times
1. Who spoke against her at this time?
2. How did some officers treat the soldiers?
3. How did Miss Nightingale feel about the soldiers?

Helping the Soldiers
1. What did she do for the soldiers?
2. Why did the soldiers bring their money to her?

Back Home
1. Why did the people of England wish to honour her?
2. How did she travel home?

After the War
1. What did she want to do for the common soldiers?
2. Why did she want to destroy her fame?

Last Days
1. How old was she when she died?
2. What is marked on her gravestone?

THREE—ABRAHAM LINCOLN

Early American Life
1. Where did the people from Europe first settle?
2. What did the people find as they moved west?

Home and School
1. Where did Abraham go to school?
2. Why wasn't the father happy in Kentucky?

Sickness and Death
1. What was the common saying about the early settlers?
2. What did the father do after his wife died?

School and Books
1. Why did Abraham have to work hard?
2. Why wasn't he very happy in his work?
3. How do we know he was strong?

Leaving Home
1. Why did the Lincoln family move to Illinois?
2. Then what did Abraham do?

Slavery in New Orleans
1. From where had the slaves been brought?
2. Why was he known as "Honest Abe"?

Fighting Indians
1. When was Lincoln free to do as he pleased?
2. What group did he join?

Abe the Store-keeper
1. Where did he and Berry get money to buy the store?
2. Why wasn't the store successful?

At the Bottom of the Barrel
1. Where did he find a book?
2. What did the book seem to say to him?

Abe the Law-maker
1. Why was he elected to the state government?
2. While in the government what was he studying?

Abe the Lawyer
1. Why was he known as an honest lawyer?
2. When did he travel around the state?

Saving a Life
1. In what serious trouble was Jack Armstrong's son?
2. When did the house-painter claim to see the blow?

3. What did Lincoln prove?

The Question of Slavery
1. In what states was slavery permitted and not permitted?
2. How did Lincoln feel about slavery?
3. What did he say no man was good enough to do?

In the White House
1. Who went with Lincoln to Washington?
2. Where did he say good-bye to his friends?
3. Why was it a difficult time to be president?

The Civil War Begins
1. Where did fighting first begin?
2. How long did the war last?
3. What did the ordinary people come to know about Lincoln?

Lincoln and the Soldier
1. Why was a young soldier ordered to be shot?
2. Where did Lincoln go?
3. How did the soldier later pay?

Freeing the Slaves
1. Why did Lincoln free the slaves?
2. How many slaves were freed?

The Gettysburg Speech
1. Why was a big meeting held at Gettysburg?
2. Why didn't Lincoln seem to succeed?

The End of the War
1. What happened in 1864?
2. What task would be before him at the end of the war?

Death
1. Who had planned to kill Lincoln and why?
2. How did the people feel about his death?

FOUR—MADAME CURIE

Introduction
1. When and where was Marya Sklodovska born?
2. What were the occupations of her father and mother?

Danger in the Classroom
1. What happened when the gateman rang the bell?
2. Why was Marya chosen to answer the questions?

The Early Years
1. How many children were there in the family?
2. What did Bronya try to do?
3. What did Marya do to bring money into the family?

The "Floating University"
1. What was the "Floating University"?
2. Why did they meet secretly?

The Governess
1. Where did Marya go to work as a governess?
2. What gave her great joy?

The Young Man
1. Why did the young man fall in love with Marya?
2. Why didn't they get married?

Back to Warsaw
1. Why did Marya leave her position?
2. What did her sister write her to do?

The Paris Home
1. Why didn't Marie continue to live in her sister's home?
2. Why did she sometimes not light the stove?

Hunger
1. Why did her sister's husband come to Marie's room?
2. What had she eaten that day?

Cold
1. Why was it sometimes difficult for her to sleep?
2. What did she do to get warm?

Her Marriage
1. Who was Pierre Curie?
2. Where did they go after they were married?

The New Home
1. How did she find time to prepare the meals?
2. What did Marie and her husband do in the evenings?

In the Laboratory
1. What did Marie the scientist set out to discover?
2. What success did she at first have?

Working Together
1. How did other scientists feel about the experiments of the Curies?
2. How long did the Curies work before they succeeded?

Unwelcome Fame
1. Why didn't the Curies enjoy fame?
2. Where and of what did men take photographs?

The Nobel Prize
1. Why couldn't they go to Sweden to receive the Prize?
2. Why was the Prize of value to them?

A Great Decision
1. Why was it against the scientific spirit to sell their secret?
2. Where did they go that afternoon?

Fame and Children
1. How many children did they now have and what were their names?
2. Where was Monsieur Curie invited to teach and why did he at first refuse?

Death of Pierre Curie
1. How was Pierre Curie killed?
2. To what new position was she appointed?

The First World War
1. What did Marie Curie do with the precious radium and why?
2. What was a "little Curie"?

Trip to America
1. Why did Madame Curie go to America and who went with her?
2. What was she expected to do in America?

Gift from America
1. What ceremony took place in Washington?
2. What did she do before the ceremony?

The Last Years
1. Where did Madame Curie spend most of her last years?
2. When did she die and where was she buried?

FIVE—ALBERT SCHWEITZER

The Fight
1. Why did the two boys want to fight?
2. What happened to George?

School Life
1. Why did the boys call him "the little gentleman"?
2. Why did he enjoy his long walks to school?
3. Why did the boys call him "Laughter"?

Love of Animals
1. What did Albert hate?
2. What weapon did his friend make?

Music
1. Why was his teacher angry when he did not practise enough?
2. What music did he enjoy most?

School Examinations
1. What happened at the examinations?
2. What did he do when having his army training?

Music Again
1. What did his aunt arrange for him to do in Paris?
2. What did Monsieur Widor think of his organ playing?

The Great Decision
1. What did Albert ask himself about his future?
2. What did he decide to do until he was thirty years old?

Studying Medicine
1. How did he pay for his studies of medicine?
2. What work was his wife trained to do?

Joseph
1. Where did Schweitzer find Joseph?

2. In what way was Joseph unusual?

Life at Lambaréné
1. What was the present which Schweitzer gave him?
2. What was one difference between the hospital at Lambaréné and the hospital at Strasbourg?

Hospital Work
1. What was the name which people gave to Schweitzer?
2. Why did they call him this?

Back in Europe
1. Why did the Schweitzers go back to France?
2. When they were set free where did the Schweitzers go?

Africa Again
1. What had happened to the hospital?
2. Why was the discovery of a spring important?

Later Years
1. When did Schweitzer die?

LIST OF NEW WORDS

Atlantic,	the ocean between Europe and America
aunt,	the wife of an uncle
Bible,	the holy book of the Christian Church
borrow,	to get the use of a thing which will be given back
cabin,	a small rough house
ceiling,	the inside roof of a room
ceremony,	a solemn meeting
certainly,	without doubt
children,	the boys and girls of a family
Christians,	people who follow the teaching of Jesus
climate,	the weather conditions of a country
concert,	a meeting for hearing music
coolie,	a man who does rough work in some countries
crash,	a loud noise made by something falling
doll,	a small play-thing made like a human being
drunken,	badly behaved because of strong drink
earning,	obtaining money for work
experiments,	work done to find new knowledge

fortunately,	by good chance
governess,	a woman whose work is to teach children in a home
hospital,	a building used for the care of sick people
ink,	coloured liquid used for writing with a pen
inner,	inside, in the mind
Koran,	the holy book of the Moslems
laboratory,	a place where experiments in science are done
lecture,	to speak in order to teach
Moslems,	people who follow the teaching of Muhammad
northern,	of the north
operate,	to cut the body in order to heal it
organ,	a large musical instrument
physics,	one kind of science
piano,	a large musical instrument
president,	the head of a government
professor,	a teacher in a university
rubber,	material which jumps back when it is pulled
sewing,	needle-work
soup,	meat and vegetables cooked in a lot of water
southern,	of the south
stove,	an enclosed fire for cooking
stripe,	long narrow mark
student,	one who studies
ticket,	a card showing that the holder has paid money
trousers,	men's clothes covering the legs
truck,	a low cart for heavy goods
turban,	a cloth covering for the head
vegetables,	plants used for food
whenever,	when at any time
wrestle,	to try to throw someone to the ground